Collins

need to know?

Buying Property in Spain

Mark Stucklin

Collins

First published in 2006 by Collins
an imprint of
HarperCollins Publishers
77–85 Fulham Palace Road
London W6 8JB

www.collins.co.uk

Collins is a registered trademark of
HarperCollins Publishers Limited.

10 09 08 07 06
6   5   4   3   2   1

A catalogue record for this book is available from the British Library

Editor: Heather Thomas
Designer: Rolando Ugolini
Series design: Mark Thomson

Photographs
The publishers would like to thank the following:
Front cover photograph: © The Travel Library
A Place in the Sun: pages 8, 68, 119, 133, 158
Campbell-Ferguson/Survey Spain: page 86
Grupo Lábaro: pages 27, 43, 147, 151
Hyatt Regency La Manga: pages 16, 52, 62, 91, 101, 114–115
La Quinta: pages 7, 72
Rob Scott/Spanish Homes Magazine: page 32
Mark Stucklin: pages 23, 35, 37, 38, 39, 41, 47, 49, 67, 79, 80, 94,
97, 105, 108, 123, 124, 125, 129, 130, 137, 141, 144, 170

ISBN-13 978 0 00 720773 2
ISBN-10 0 00 720773 5

Colour reproduction by Colourscan, Singapore
Printed and bound by Printing Express Ltd, Hong Kong

Publisher's note
All figures quoted are the most up-to-date currently available
and are correct and representative at the time of going to press,
but should be treated as a rough guide only as the Spanish
property market is subject to rapid and frequent change.

Contents

Introduction

Buying a property in Spain can be very enriching, both financially and in terms of enhancing your happiness and quality of life. However, this will only be the case if you get the purchase right.

This means buying the right property for the right reasons and in the right way. You have to approach your purchase in a structured and organized fashion whilst understanding the process and property market in Spain. You need to be aware of the risks involved in making one of the biggest investments of your life in a foreign country, whilst dealing with people who do not necessarily have your best interests at heart. Most of all, it means being well informed at all times, as information is power, and the more you know, the harder it is for others to take advantage of you. This book is designed to arm you with the know-how you need to achieve this objective so that you can safely buy a Spanish property.

It follows that the purpose of this book is not to 'sell the dream' but to point out the risks and realities of pursuing the dream. This inevitably means focusing on the problems, costs and other negative issues that may make you wonder whether buying a property in Spain is really such a good idea after all. That is certainly a question you should ask yourself, as for some people the answer will be *'no'* and it is better to find this out before proceeding to buy. However, for the majority of British people who dream of owning a property in the beautiful surroundings and sunshine of Spain there is no good reason why they shouldn't, and this book is not intended to shoot down any realistic dreams. Instead, it focuses on how to avoid the problems in order to help you keep out of harm's way when buying in Spain. Don't let these pages dampen your enthusiasm if your dreams are realistic; forewarned is forearmed, and you can find and purchase a property in the sun that will suit your individual needs and fulfil your dream.

1 Where to buy in Spain

Wherever you buy in Spain there is no escaping the fact that property is no longer as cheap as it used to be. Spanish property prices have risen dramatically over the last five to 10 years, and sterling has lost value compared to the euro (and what was the peseta) over the same period, making Spanish property more expensive for British buyers. However, prices vary considerably between regions, meaning that a villa on the Costa Blanca or in Murcia might be cheaper than the average apartment on the western stretch of the Costa del Sol. British buyers should choose the region that best suits their overall needs and budget.

Spanish property prices

British property prices have risen even more dramatically than Spanish ones, so relative to property in the UK, Spanish property is still reasonably cheap. However, in absolute terms, it is much more expensive to buy in Spain than it used to be.

Sustainability
Several international institutions have questioned the sustainability of recent property price increases in Spain, and 84 per cent of Spaniards think that Spain is suffering from a property price bubble.

Property market performance

It is important to realize from the very outset that you cannot set off for Spain nowadays hoping to buy a good-quality villa in an attractive area for a song. That used to be possible a decade or more ago, but those days are long gone and it sometimes appears as if foreign buyers have not yet taken this on board. Before moving onto examining whereabouts in Spain to buy, let's have a quick look at how the Spanish property market has performed in recent years.

Spanish property prices have increased in nominal terms (before adjusting for inflation) every year since 1993. In real terms, prices have increased every year since 1997. However, the most dramatic price increases have taken place more recently, with double-digit percentage price rises in each year from 1999 to the end of 2004. To give you an example, in 2004 average Spanish property prices increased by 17.3 per cent, and by 17.5 per cent in 2003. This means that Spanish property was 107 per cent more expensive in 2005 than it was five years previously (more than double), and 150 per cent more expensive than it was in 1996.

Regional price rises

The figures mentioned above are the Spanish government's average figures for the market as a whole. If you look at the Spanish property market region by region, you find that prices have risen across the board, but more so in some places than in others. The table opposite shows how property prices have risen in a selection of regions; in the absence of the latest figures, which have not been released yet at the time of going to press, price rises are given up to the end of 2004 to illustrate the ongoing trend.

Over the last five years prices have risen the most in Murcia (169 per cent), followed by Andalusia (132 per cent), the Valencian region (124 per cent) and the Balearics (111 per cent). Generally speaking, Spanish property prices have risen the most in those coastal areas where foreigners, especially the British, tend to buy, although they have also risen substantially in the big cities Barcelona and Madrid.

What does all this signify? It means that unless you want to buy property in one of Spain's inland regions, such as Teruel or Extremadura, you will have to deal with relatively high prices, although some coastal areas, e.g. Murcia, are still much cheaper than others, such as Catalonia and the Balearics. If a property in a sought-after coastal area is very cheap (relative to the market) there is usually a good reason for this, and one that should make you think twice before buying.

After so many years of increases, Spanish property prices might now start to stagnate, or even fall slightly in coastal areas where the supply of new properties has exploded. This could affect its investment potential, so it is unrealistic to expect your villa to provide you with a home and an exceptional investment in the short-term. However, in the long-term, over 10 to 15 years, Spanish property should still be a good investment, as it is

Property price trends

Average price by autonomous region Source: *Ministerio de Vivienda*

Year	National		Andalusia		Catalonia		Valencia		Galicia		Balearics		Canaries		Murcia	
	€/m2	+/-%	€/m2	+/-%	€/m2	+/-%	€/m2	+/-%	€/m2	+/-%	€/m2	+/-%	€/m2	+/-%	€/m2	+/-%
2000	907	15%	663	13%	1.171	16%	659	13%	661	8%	1.153	23%	963	17%	538	12%
2001	1.021	13%	790	19%	1.297	11%	790	20%	748	13%	1.366	18%	1.127	17%	708	32%
2002	1.191	17%	950	20%	1.497	15%	924	17%	832	11%	1.514	12%	1.247	11%	845	19%
2003	1.400	18%	1.129	19%	1.779	19%	1.085	17%	923	11%	1.718	13%	1.349	8%	1.018	20%
2004	1.642	17%	1.363	21%	2.119	19%	1.304	20%	1.037	12%	1.975	15%	1.489	10%	1.289	27%

likely that millions of Northern Europeans will retire to Spain over this period to enjoy its lovely climate and surroundings, unique culture, lower cost of living and higher quality of life.

Deciding where to buy

The relative prices of property in different regions and on different coasts will play a part in your decision on where to buy. However, most people have a good reason for choosing a particular place or region – they may

Provinces of Spain

have spent holidays there or have family and friends who live there. If you have no compelling reason for choosing a specific area, you may have to visit several and explore all the possibilities until you find the one that suits you best.

Opinions of Spain's different regions are highly subjective and depend upon people's tastes. Some find the heat and year-round uniformity of the climate on the Costa del Sol unbearable and prefer the milder climate, seasonal variations and greenery of Catalonia. Others find Catalonia too cold in the winter and prefer the dry air, desertscape and endless sunshine of Murcia. Everyone has their own preferences.

Buyers who are open-minded need to clarify their priorities, such as climate, development, services, community and prices, and then research potential regions in depth, including making visits. The table on page 14 lists the advantages of the main regions and may help you to focus your search. Here is a brief overview of the five most popular regions in Spain.

Catalonia

The Costa Brava, north of Barcelona, is one of Spain's most beautiful and unspoilt Mediterranean coastlines, where the hills run down from the Pyrenees into the sea and hide pretty coves and sandy white beaches. The Costa Dorada, to the south of Barcelona, is flatter, with long sandy beaches, but is more over-developed. Inland the countryside is green with well-kept farms, orchards and vineyards or natural parks. However, Catalonia has colder winters and shorter summers than, say, the Costa del Sol. It can also be a difficult region for expatriates to establish a social life.

Valencia

The autonomous region of Valencia, being long and thin and running north to south, has a varied coastline that changes noticeably near Benidorm, south of which the landscape turns increasingly arid. The coast north of Valencia tends to be overlooked by Brits, most of whom focus on the area around Denia and Javea, which is attractive and green with a solid expatriate community, or the area south of Alicante, which, although overdeveloped and arid, does offer cheap housing and sunshine.

Where to buy

COSTA BRAVA Catalonia

Near Barcelona; good infrastructure; reasonably well-controlled development in most areas; proximity to South of France; Catalonia is the most efficiently run region of Spain; noticeable change of seasons, but winter mild and sunny; excellent beaches; excellent golf; great variety in surroundings; rich local culture and cuisine; skiing in the Pyrenees.
PRICES: Mid to high (Barcelona factor)

COSTA DORADA Catalonia

Near Barcelona; good infrastructure; areas close to Barcelona heavily developed, but further south development is lighter; Catalonia is most efficiently run region of Spain; excellent beaches; limited but reasonable golf course selection; beautiful wine regions; mild winters; good family location: theme parks and beaches; Ebro Delta nature reservation; rich local culture.
PRICES: Mid range

BALEARICS Mallorca

Large international community; very beautiful coast and countryside; mild climate but noticeable seasonal variations; excellent beaches; fantastic marinas and water sports facilities; strict environmental controls; further development is restricted; glamour factor, upmarket; high-quality rural property stock, and general quality of housing stock high (German influence).
PRICES: High

COSTA BLANCA Valencian Region

Good year-round climate; large international community; excellent beaches; central location for trips to north and south; wide range of activities and entertainment; large range of properties and developments on offer; great variety in surroundings; good family location.
PRICES: High on the north coast; cheaper on the south coast

COSTA CALIDA Murcia

Very dry climate; region in development; cheap cost of living; more a retirement than a family location.
PRICES: Cheap

COSTA DEL SOL Andalusia

Fantastic climate; large international community; largest selection of golf courses in Spain; glamour appeal; enormous selection of properties and developments; good international services and facilities; skiing in Sierra Nevada; tourist opportunities.
PRICES: Medium to high on the west coast; medium on the east coast

COSTA DE LA LUZ Andalusia

Good climate, though cooler and windier than Costa del Sol; not over-developed; more of 'real Spain' on offer; fantastic beaches.
PRICES: Mid range

CANARIES

The best winter sun destination in Europe; extraordinary variety of climates and countryside; lower property purchase taxes; consolidated international community.
PRICES: Mid range

Murcia

This has only emerged as a serious destination for non-Spanish buyers in the last few years, but with the local government's support for residential development, it looks likely to consolidate its growing status as a foreign homebuyer's destination. The landscape is arid but dramatic, and property prices and the cost of living are very reasonable. A lack of water is Murcia's big challenge for the future.

Andalusia

Home to the Costa del Sol, Costa de la Luz and the lesser known Costa de Almeria, Andalusia is one of Spain's biggest regions with an astonishing wealth of landscapes, micro-climates and cultural attractions. Most British expatriates and other nationalities live on the Costa del Sol, between Malaga and Gibraltar, drawn there by the warm year-round climate, golf and well-developed industry catering to expatriates. It will always be the favourite destination of British buyers.

Balearics

Although Menorca, Ibiza and Formentera are all in their own way highly attractive, the biggest and most popular island of all with the northern European buyers is Mallorca (Majorca). Generally an upmarket destination, with prices to match, both the interior and the coast are stunning, and the island is increasingly becoming a relocation, rather than simply a holiday destination.

want to know more?

Take it to the next level...

▶ **Types of property** 34
▶ **Doing the research** 54
▶ **Examining your needs** 58

Other sources...

▶ Look in monthly magazines, such as *Everything Spain*. Most are available from local newsagents.
▶ For up-to-date stories and information on the Spanish property market, look in *The Sunday Times* Home section.
▶ For market reports and property guides to the Spanish regions, see www.spanishpropertyinsight.com

2 How the market works

When you are buying property in Spain, it helps to understand how the Spanish property market works. This means identifying the key participants in the business and looking at how they operate and the value they offer. The more that you know about the business the easier it is for you to select appropriate companies to deal with, and the harder it becomes for anyone to take advantage of you. Let's take an in-depth look at the different types of companies you will be confronted with when you are buying a Spanish property. Choosing the right one is the key to a successful purchase.

Estate agents

Spanish buyers often use word of mouth or private advertisements to find property. Most British buyers, however, rely upon British estate agents working in Spain, whom they trust to help them make one of the most expensive purchases of their lives. The problem is that many of these agents are not trustworthy.

Be cautious

There is no doubt that estate agents can provide an extremely valuable service if they are ethical, competent and professional. Unfortunately, many of the agents that British buyers end up dealing with fail to meet one or more of these conditions. It is essential to avoid incompetent and unscrupulous estate agents when buying a property. Some of the biggest risks that buyers run can be traced back to the competence and attitude of estate agents, and many have seen their dreams shattered.

There are several reasons why the professional standards of estate agents in Spain are so low, especially amongst the British, Irish and other foreign agents whom British buyers tend to end up dealing with. Firstly, anyone can now play the role of intermediary in property transactions since the Spanish government deregulated the market in 2000. This means that Brits and other foreigners with no experience of the market, no professional training and not a word of Spanish can legally sell property in Spain. Previously, membership of one of Spain's professional real estate associations (API and GIPE) was a legal requirement for anyone selling property, which meant professional training and some level of professional indemnity. Whilst this system was not perfect, and many of the foreigners selling Spanish property ignored it or found ways around it, it did at least set a standard and ensured that anyone legally selling property had professional training and understood the relevant documentation in Spanish. Now it is an officially sanctioned free-for-all.

Another unfortunate reality of the Spanish property business, especially the foreign buyer sector, is that high commissions and low regulations have attracted people with a greedy timeshare mentality of aggressive and unethical sales. This is no coincidence; as timeshare collapsed, freehold property sales boomed, and many former timeshare sales people moved into property. As a consequence, the business is infested with greed, pressure-selling techniques and professional incompetence.

There are other factors that help depress professional standards: high commissions of between five and 35 per cent or more that attract many unprofessional agents and allow them to survive on the back of even just a few sales a year; the one-off nature of the business, where clients only buy once so their repeat business is not important; and the fact that buyers cannot always get the information they need to make informed decisions. And size is no guide to quality: some of the biggest

Rural Andalusia has several beautiful lakes that can be enjoyed in summer. In some places, new developments and golf courses are being constructed around these lakes.

foreign-run agents to have emerged in Spain over the last decade or so are also among the most unscrupulous and aggressive companies.

Anyone planning to buy a property needs to be aware of this situation. They need to know that, due to incompetence or a lack of scruples, many of the British companies and individuals selling Spanish property can't be trusted to help them invest a substantial part of their savings. Buyers should make an effort to find those companies that can be trusted. Fortunately, there are many professional, competent and ethical agents in the market, but the challenge is knowing how to find them (see below).

Different types of agents

Having explained why buyers need to be cautious when deciding on which properties and individuals to deal with, let's look at the different types of estate agents and property brokers operating in Spain.

Spanish estate agents

Many Spanish estate agents (known as *Agentes de la Propiedad Inmobiliaria*, or APIs) focus on a local Spanish clientele and don't have English-speaking staff to deal with British buyers. There are exceptions, especially on the coast, but on the whole Brits will find it easier to deal with British owned-and-run agents operating in Spain than Spanish agents. This is a shame because, generally, Spanish agents are more knowledgeable about the local market and conveyancing process than are the new breed of British agents. They may also have a different portfolio of properties from Spanish vendors.

Foreign owned-and-run estate agents

The number of foreign owned-and-run estate agents in Spain has exploded in the last 10 years. They vary from one person working out of a car with a mobile phone and a website, to big companies with hundreds of staff, enormous advertising budgets and a year-round programme of UK property exhibitions. The smaller agencies tend to focus on the market in their immediate areas, whilst bigger companies might have several offices, even covering different coasts. Some have opened a sales office in the UK. Some of these companies are excellent and some are dreadful.

Corredores (independent brokers)

In many rural areas, *corredores* still play a key role in the property market. They are often well-known figures in the community, and local people will approach them when they want to sell a property. The *corredor* will then find a buyer, often working through local estate agents or buyer's agents. Their fees are usually modest, charging both buyer and seller one to two per cent when the sale is made. A common problem is that many of them do not speak English.

Multi-listing networks in Spain

Many estate agencies in Spain participate in networks through which they share clients, properties and commissions. Agency A may have a buyer but not the right property, whereas Agency B has the property but not the buyer. Therefore they collaborate and make the sale, splitting the commission. The problem here is that commissions are high as at least two agencies and the network company need to earn a commission from the sale, whilst participating agencies have an incentive to withhold their best properties from the network.

Virtual property sales companies

The internet has spawned a new type of business that can be described as 'virtual' property sales companies. These appear to be estate agents, but in reality they are just websites that market a selection of properties from various estate agents in return for part of the commission. Buyers are better off dealing directly with local agents than through such intermediaries.

UK-based agents selling Spanish property

A brief mention should also be made of UK-based estate agents trying to sell Spanish property, usually through partner agents in Spain. However, you always need to deal with local people who know what they are talking about, so in many cases these companies don't add any value, unless, of course, they have a branch in Spain.

Promoters

If the Spanish property market has been hot in recent years then the market for new developments has been white-hot. High profits in a booming market have sucked in many new entrants and the 'costas' are now awash with promoters, most of them Spanish but with an increasing number of foreign developers, too.

What they do

The majority of promoters (*promotores*) are small companies with one or two developments, but in coastal areas where the British tend to buy it is common to find big promoters with major projects which often include golf courses.

Promoters are the risk-takers who put together and finance a development, mainly through bank borrowing and from the deposits taken from buyers for off-plan properties. Although all but the biggest promoters contract out the design and construction of the development, it is always the promoter who determines its overall quality and the way in which clients are treated. Estate agents may not stick around to help buyers deal with the promoter, often disappearing as soon as the sale is made and the commission in the bank. This means that clients have to work closely with the promoters they buy from, and a promoter's attitude to business will largely determine how well things turn out for buyers.

Quality and performance

The standards of quality and performance will vary widely from developer to developer and from region to region. Unfortunately for British buyers, some of the worst developers target them, as they are much easier to take advantage of than their Spanish counterparts and put up less of a fight in a dispute. Be aware that badly managed, unethical, greedy or simply incompetent developers exist and are over-represented in the areas where the British tend to buy. It is important to avoid these kinds of promoters, and size is not necessarily any guide to quality.

However, there are also many excellent Spanish developers, large and small, offering new promotions in areas that appeal to the British. The problem lies in distinguishing the good from the bad, and British buyers are at a disadvantage when it comes to researching developers in Spain. It is easier for people who live there and speak Spanish than it is for foreigners. Many British buyers make no attempt to look into the reputation and the background of promoters. However, before buying on a new development, you should always do your own research on the promoter and should not rely on the agent from whom you buy for all your information.

The garden of a town house in Begur on the Costa Brava. A pretty garden and pool look great but remember they are high maintenance.

Other property companies

Estate agents play a key role for British buyers and they have the lion's share of the market, but they are not the only companies that are involved in selling Spanish property. Let's look at some of the other companies that can help you to buy property in Spain.

Buyer's agents

These are paid by and work exclusively for buyers. They search for properties on behalf of their clients but, unlike search and find companies (opposite), they do not receive commission from estate agents. This means their incentives are completely transparent and their clients don't have to worry about them pushing properties that pay the highest commission. Furthermore, they are not limited in what they can find for their clients by commission-sharing agreements with estate agents and are free to search for properties from private sellers who don't pay any commissions. This is a big advantage in a country like Spain, where many Spaniards, especially in rural areas, avoid selling their homes through estate agents. This means that buyer's agents have access to a wider selection of properties than anyone else.

Buyer's agents charge their clients a successful search fee, typically around two-and-a-half per cent of the value of the property. They also charge an upfront fee to ensure that clients are serious and to contribute to the costs of unsuccessful searches. Some people are tempted to see the fee as an extra cost, but in reality, buyer's agents are more likely to drive down the overall cost of the purchase whilst significantly increasing the buyer's chances of finding the property best suited to them. Another advantage for purchasers is that buyer's agents do not have to fight for a commission built into the sales price, which frees them to help their clients negotiate the lowest price possible for the property. They can also give genuinely unbiased advice to their clients and are likely to have more knowledge of the local property market than anyone else.

Search and find

These are not estate agents and do not have a portfolio of properties to sell. Instead they search the properties offered by a number of local agents on behalf of their clients. They arrange a shortlist of properties for clients to view, and if a sale is made they receive part of the estate agent's commission. Clients are usually charged an upfront fee to start a search and to cover the costs of unsuccessful searches. However, the fee is normally refunded to clients who end up buying through them.

Experienced search and find consultants with the right contacts can help you to find suitable properties, but do bear in mind that, unlike buyer's agents (opposite), who are paid by and work exclusively for buyers, these people charge the vendor, so they are not paid to look after your interests.

Introducers

There are many people sitting on bar stools on the coast who try to make a living as 'introducers'. They befriend potential buyers from Britain who are out visiting and introduce them to estate agents. In return, they expect to receive a part of the estate agent's commission if the client ends up buying a property through them.

Introducers claim to know who the 'trustworthy' agents are, which is why most people go along with their proposals. However, in many cases their claims are spurious and they have no interest other than to earn the highest commission possible for the minimum effort. They are more likely to recommend aggressive agents who charge high commissions or who increase the commission to pay the introducer.

Anyone who is thinking of buying a property in Spain should seek out recommendations from their friends and acquaintances who already live there, but they should always avoid being 'introduced' to estate agents or developers by strangers, who are more likely to be motivated by high commissions rather than by any desire to help.

Lawyers and mortgage brokers

Property transactions in Spain, as anywhere, are essentially a legal matter concerning the transfer of property rights from the vendor to a buyer. Relatively complex legal issues lie at the heart of every transaction and buyers should use qualified professionals to ensure that their interests are protected.

Choosing the right lawyer (*abogado*)

Without qualified legal advice, you will be taking a very large and almost entirely avoidable risk with one of the biggest investments that you will ever make. A significant number of British people who have bought in Spain complain that their lawyers were an expensive obstacle rather than a solution to their problems. Some complain of inept lawyers and assert that you are better off doing the legal work yourself with the help of a translator. Others have decided that lawyers are not worth their fees and that a *gestor* (a less qualified administrator) can provide the same level of protection but at a significantly lower cost. Most unfortunate of all are the non-Spanish buyers who have found that their lawyers worked against them due to hidden conflicts of interests.

Despite these negative experiences, you should always use a lawyer. Without a competent and independent lawyer, you run considerable risks, and given the sums of money at stake it just is not worth it. However, you have to choose the right one as all the problems with lawyers can be traced back either to incompetence or conflicts of interest.

Conflicts of interest

Very few British buyers have a Spanish lawyer in their address book when they set out to buy a property. Given that many estate agents make a song and dance of providing legal solutions, most British buyers take the easy option and use the lawyer being pushed under their noses. However, by doing so they run the risk of hiring the very lawyers from whom they will need protection if a dispute arises.

Lawyers who are recommended by estate agents and developers come in different guises. Some companies will offer their own in-house lawyers, who will draw up contracts in the interests of the company and fight its corner if push comes to shove. You are probably better off doing all the legal work yourself with the help of a Spanish-English dictionary than using an in-house lawyer.

It is more likely that estate agents will recommend a lawyer who is nominally independent from them. In many cases the independence will be genuine and the recommended lawyer

The beautiful and dramatic coastline of the Costa Brava in Catalonia is popular with British buyers.

will look after the buyer's interests. However, in some cases there is just a veneer of independence that covers up murky commercial relationships and conflicts of interests. Buyers are lulled into a false sense of security whilst the recommended lawyer does little more than oil the wheels of the transaction on the estate agent's behalf. Even when recommended lawyers are genuinely independent from estate agents there is usually some sort of business relationship that can put lawyers under pressure to cut corners.

So when buying property in Spain you need to find a lawyer who is working for you and you alone, and avoid using one who is recommended by estate agents or developers. Looking for an independent lawyer once a dispute has started is like closing the stable door after the horse has bolted. You need your own lawyer from the very start.

Finding a competent, independent lawyer

If you are serious about buying property in Spain you should make your search for a lawyer one of your very first tasks. This gives you time to find an English-speaking lawyer with no connection to the company you buy from, which reduces the risks of hidden commercial relationships that might undermine the service you receive. It also means you have your own lawyer on hand to check the very first contracts you are expected to sign.

A sensible approach is to ask your friends and acquaintances for recommendations. If this draws a blank, consider contacting the British consulate in or closest to the region where you are buying. They can email or fax you a list of English-speaking lawyers in the region. Many English-speaking Spanish lawyers also advertise in the press or can be found through internet searches. It does not really matter how you find your lawyer, so long as they are working for you.

Choose a local lawyer

If possible you should hire a lawyer based in Spain, and preferably in the region where you are buying. Locally-based lawyers can easily visit the town hall of the municipality and may even know the mayor, the municipal architect and the local Notary. In Spain, where contacts count, this can be a big advantage when sorting out problems. Local lawyers are also more likely to know about regional urban plans, the problems specific to the region, and the reputations of local estate agents and developers. They are on site to do legal checks and can readily accompany you to the signing of the deeds before a Notary. Lawyers who are not locally based have to operate over the phone or through associates, all of which may reduce their speed and effectiveness whilst increasing the cost to you. However, there are instances where British buyers are better off using Spanish lawyers based in major cities, such as Barcelona, Madrid or even London. This is usually the case when buyers need a high level of international fiscal expertise, or where an appropriate local lawyer cannot be found.

Use a specialist

Spanish lawyers specialize in different areas of law and ideally you need one who has real estate law expertise (*derecho inmobiliario*). In theory, a generalist or even a divorce lawyer can help you buy a

This beautiful *masia*, set in its manicured gardens, is a Catalan country house.

property but in practice the service will not be as good. This largely explains why some British buyers have found their lawyers to be incompetent. Bear in mind that the lists of lawyers provided by British consulates and other sources do not normally indicate areas of specialization so you should always look into this before proceeding with a lawyer.

Dealing with lawyers

You need to establish a good working relationship which is built on trust, and avoid giving any impression that you lack confidence in your lawyer. However, always keep copies of all the important documents you pass to your lawyer and make notes of conversations and decisions.

Many lawyers charge between one and one-and-a-half per cent of the value of a property for their legal services, whilst others charge on an hourly basis or a flat fee (all fees attract VAT at 16 per cent). Just be warned that there are considerable variations in fees and fee structures. Make sure that you ask for the fees to be explained and for an estimate of the hours involved, but also be diplomatic when discussing fees, as Spanish lawyers do not like to be haggled with.

Typically you will be asked to pay a provision of funds of 1,000 euros or up to 50 per cent of the fee when your lawyer starts working for you, with the remainder due once your purchase is completed. You should expect to receive a receipt for your initial payment that details the amount and the purpose of your payment.

If things go wrong

If you have doubts about your lawyer, you have the right to change him/her at any time. To do this, all you need do is to send a letter or fax informing them of your decision and giving instructions to pass your file to your new lawyer by a certain date. If your instructions are ignored, then you should send an ultimatum threatening to complain to the local lawyers association (*colegio de abogados*) and then do so in the last resort.

If you change lawyers during the purchase you only have to pay for work provided up to that date. It is difficult to measure the work done and, most likely, you will just have to settle for not making any further payments.

Choosing a mortgage broker

With mortgage interest rates in Spain (euro-zone) so low in recent years, many if not most British people will take out a Spanish mortgage (*hipoteca*). It is impossible to predict what will happen in the long term, but while UK mortgage rates remain significantly higher than in the euro-zone, most British buyers will continue to be better off taking out a Spanish mortgage. Some financial institutions in the UK are starting to offer euro-mortgages, but the conditions tend to be less attractive than is typical in Spain, although this may change.

Although an increasing number of Spanish banks (and foreign banks in Spain) are targeting British buyers with their mortgages, most people will find it easier to work with a mortgage broker who can help them shop around for the best deal and manage the mortgage arrangement process in English.

Specialist brokers are to be found in both Spain and the UK. They nearly always charge a fee for a successful mortgage, which may vary from a half to two per cent, and many also charge an upfront fee to consider an application – variously called a study fee, application fee or administration fee.

Mortgage brokers can play a key role in a successful purchase, so it is important to find an experienced, competent and efficient broker with access to the full range of mortgage lenders in Spain. Be aware that some brokers lack experience and charge relatively high fees whilst offering a limited range of mortgages. It is worth researching and comparing different brokers before committing to one. Brokers based in Spain are usually in a better position to shop around on behalf of their clients than those who are based in the UK.

want to know more?

Take it to the next level...

▶ **Doing the research** 54
▶ **Preparing yourself** 64
▶ **Selecting companies** 74

Other sources...
▶ **The British Embassy in Madrid offers advice to people moving to Spain: www.ukinspain.com**
▶ **For more information on professional organizations of estate agents (in Spanish), see: www.consejocoapis.org and www.gipe.es**
▶ ***Colegios de Abogados* is a directory of local legal associations (in Spanish): www.cgae.es**
▶ **Mortgage information can be accessed at the Spanish Mortgage Association: www.ahe.es**
▶ **Spanish language speakers can view the website of the Spanish Government's Consumer Protection Department at: www.consumo-inc.es**

3 Types of property

You need to analyze your requirements with a
view to producing a detailed brief that describes
the property you want. Before doing that it will
help to have an overview of the different types
of property available, as realistic expectations
are always important when it comes to buying
property. The 'dream' property that you have
in your mind's eye might not be the most
practical, nor the one that most enhances your
quality of life. You need to establish what type
of property is best for you and your circumstances.

Which property is best?

A wide choice of different types of property is on offer in Spain, and before rushing into making a purchase, you should think very carefully about what will be best for your individual needs. Size, location, local facilities and budget will all be important considerations when you are making your decision.

Modern villas
Modern villas that were built during the last 20 years are often better laid out and easier to maintain than older properties.

Villas

Villas are modern detached properties with a garden and pool. They represent an irresistible mix of comfort, privacy and space, setting the stage for living the good life. Therefore it is not surprising that villas are the most sought-after type of Spanish property amongst British buyers – their dream home.

Is a villa right for you?

Although they make good permanent or semi-permanent homes, especially for families with children and pets, villas may not suit everyone in terms of practicality. They are not ideal 'lock and leave' properties and this factor should be considered by anyone looking for a holiday home.

They are relatively large properties with gardens and often a private pool, all of which means constant maintenance and cleaning, with their corresponding costs. Being large and relatively expensive, they will also attract higher municipal and government taxes than smaller properties, driving up overheads. Buying a villa also makes it more likely that you will have to get in the car to go anywhere, as the majority are on residential developments (*urbanización* – see page 46), away from town centres. What villas there are close to the centre of towns or villages are highly sought after and command a price premium.

Although most villas, especially those built over the last few decades, are on residential developments, they can also exist

This modern villa is on an urbanization. These developments offer many benefits and services to buyers of both holiday and permanent homes.

independently of urbanizations (as residential developments are known in Spain). However, detached properties built on urbanizations often benefit from being part of a secure gated community and have access to a range of communal facilities. In Valencia, villas on urbanizations are also protected from any issues related to the 'land grab' law (see page 50). Putting aside questions of taste and looking at it from a purely practical point of view, villas on residential developments probably offer the best overall solution.

Apartments

After detached properties, apartments (*pisos y apartamentos*) are the next most sought-after type of property amongst British buyers. In towns and cities, all along the coast, and increasingly on golf developments, there is a wide selection of apartments to choose from. They have always been the backbone of the Spanish property market – much more so than in the UK – and the only place you will not find them is deep in the countryside.

Is an apartment right for you?

Apartments do not make ideal principal homes for families with children and pets, although Spanish families, escaping as many of them do to their second homes at weekends, seem quite comfortable living in them. Apartments do make for perfect 'lock and leave' holiday homes, being easier and cheaper to manage than detached or semi-detached properties. They also suit elderly people who are looking for a convenient and secure home in a pleasant part of the world. Some apartments have access to communal gardens and pools, which are perfect for enjoying the Spanish climate as well as cutting down on hard work and maintenance costs. Being close to other owners also increases your security, but on the downside noise can be a problem as many Spanish apartments have thin dividing walls through which sound travels easily.

An apartment block with a modernist façade in Barcelona. City life is a popular option for increasing numbers of buyers.

Modern semi-detached properties

In the past, semi-detached properties (*casas adosadas*) were mainly to be found in towns and villages. However, in recent times demand has grown amongst both Spaniards and foreigners for modern semi-detached properties on new developments, a trend that will continue as people find that semis deliver many of the benefits of villas but at a more reasonable overall cost (both of purchase and maintenance).

Is a semi right for you?

Modern semis are often built on two floors, with a private garden and perhaps room for a small swimming pool. They offer more varied living space than apartments, but are more manageable than villas. They may also share communal areas, such as gardens and a pool, with surrounding properties. They can offer a good mix of space, privacy, outside areas and communal facilities, whilst being easier and cheaper to administer than are

As shown here, some new developments try to create a village atmosphere.

larger, detached properties. Given the communal aspect of semi-detached properties, they also offer greater security to owners and facilitate their access to a residential community.

Despite growing demand, they are still the least common type of property in Spain. They are not yet a ubiquitous fixture of modern developments, which means there is less of a choice. However, buyers will find a reasonable choice of modern semis in most of Spain's popular regions.

Village houses and town houses

Until recently the British tended to buy villas and apartments on the coast or rural properties inland, such as country cottages or old farmhouses. However, over the past 10 years, a growing number of people who want to experience the real flavour of the country and its lifestyle have been buying houses in Spain's attractive villages (*pueblos*) and inland towns, often in the old quarters where it is increasingly easy to find restored properties.

These restored town houses are in Lorca, Murcia. Some buyers prefer to live in an urban setting rather than an urbanization or in the countryside.

Is a village/town house right for you?

Most village properties tend to be semi-detached town houses (*casa de pueblo*) with small private gardens at the back but probably no room for a pool. Such properties are likely to have been built in a bygone era, and in many cases will need substantial restoration to bring them up to modern standards. Kitchens and bathrooms nearly always have to be refurbished, and it is not uncommon to find that these properties have bizarre internal distributions, small dark rooms and tiny windows. Modern installations, such as central heating or air conditioning, are rarely present, and parking is often a problem. However, there is nearly always a solution to these problems, although the bigger the solution required, the higher the cost. There is also an increasing number of restored village properties on the market.

The attraction of these properties is that they are often in pleasant surroundings, within walking distance of many of the facilities you need, and part of a Spanish rather than an expat community. Bear in mind, though, that property management companies may be harder to find in villages in the interior than on the coast.

Country houses and farmhouses

Many people dream of owning a Spanish country property - called *cortijos* in the south of Spain and *masias* in Catalonia - surrounded by citrus trees, olive groves, almond blossom and rural tranquillity. Recently, more and more people seem to be doing something about it, forsaking the crush, bustle and high prices of the coast and buying up *cortijos* inland.

Until quite recently, rural properties have been very cheap. Changes in Spanish society meant that the young and able headed for the cities whilst the country was left to a dwindling number of rural workers and the old. Times change and now affluent Spaniards returning from the cities and foreign buyers from all over Europe are looking for Spanish country properties. Prices have risen as a consequence. Country properties are still cheaper than coastal properties, and in some areas, for instance Teruel and Extremadura, rural properties are still cheap by any standards. However, looking to the future we can expect demand for country properties to rise whilst the supply will remain limited by building regulations in rural areas.

Is a country house right for you?

Country properties make for idyllic primary residences if you can cope with the potential isolation and the realities of rural living. This question needs careful consideration before committing to buy in the Spanish countryside. A good number of people have found their dreams of sitting out on a sunlit veranda enjoying sublime country views are not enough to compensate for the inconveniences of rural life with nothing much to do.

Managing a rural property in a foreign environment with language barriers can also wear owners down. A rural property may be perfect for you but it depends upon the life you expect to lead, the social life you will need and your character. It also makes for a high-maintenance holiday home that can prove complicated to manage from abroad. Perhaps more than for any other type of property, serious research and soul searching needs to be done before proceeding to buy a country house.

Country properties offer rural tranquillity but are not the most convenient to live in.

There are many types of country properties to choose from and the choice will vary substantially from region to region. For instance, there are grand country mansions in Catalonia, beautiful farmhouses in the Balearics, and quaint cottages at the end of dusty tracks in Andalusia and Extremadura. Many of them will need refurbishment, and when buying country property, you have to pay special attention to issues such as utilities, septic tanks, water rights, hunting rights, rights of way, forest fire risks and boundaries. Title deeds can also be a problem in some rural areas where properties have traditionally changed hands without any reference to the land registry.

Property condition

As well as deciding on which type of property you want, you also have to consider the state of readiness for occupation that you are prepared to accept. You have three basic choices: to buy an off-plan, newly-built or resale (previously-owned) property.

Buying off-plan

Buying property off-plan (*sobre plano*) has been very popular amongst British buyers in recent years, although many off-plan buyers have been speculative investors rather than 'end users'. Nevertheless, many end users also choose to buy off-plan, mainly due to the price advantage this option offers.

Apartments and semi-detached properties

Most off-plan buyers opt for an apartment or a semi-detached property that forms part of a developer's project, the plans for which will have already been finalized and approved by the municipal authorities. If this type of property suits you, then the key advantage (in theory) to buying off-plan is that you get a brand new property at a discount to the finished article.

However, you will have to wait for it to be built, which in unproblematic cases normally takes between 14 and 18 months. Developers who sell off-plan benefit from lower risks and access to your capital during construction, in return for which you should get a discount of anything between 10 and 20 per cent off the current market price for a comparable just-built property. In some cases, developers allow buyers a limited say over the style in which the property is finished - colours, floorings and certain fixtures, for example - as opposed to finished properties which have to be bought 'as is' with no scope for building in your own tastes from the start. However, in most cases developers don't allow off-plan buyers to make changes to plans and specifications.

Disadvantages

Committing yourself to buying something that is not yet built creates uncertainties that can turn into problems between the time of signing contracts and delivery of the property. These problems can be particularly acute for overseas buyers.

For a start you have to visualize your purchase based on plans and specifications, and the finished property might not be what you were expecting. Detailed plans and specifications, leaving little room for confusion or doubt, need to form part of a watertight contract between you and the developer if you are to avoid these problems. Many off-plan buyers have complained that the property they were delivered did not correspond to the original plans they were shown, or was delivered very late or, in the worst case scenario, has never even been started.

Many developers often provide off-plan buyers with computer-generated images of how the development will look when finished.

Detached properties

These can also be purchased off-plan from developers, with many of the same advantages and risks as described above. Due to the developer's lower economies of scale when building this sort of property, the price advantage may be smaller, but on the plus side you are likely to have more influence over the plans.

Buying a detached property off-plan from a Spanish developer involves choosing a plot and defining the plans and specifications of the property to be built on it. Bear in mind that land sales in Spain attract VAT at 16 per cent whilst new homes are taxed at seven per cent. To avoid paying the higher rate for the plot you may have to wait until the property has been completed before signing the Notarized deeds of sale. This is entirely legal, and most developers will allow you to structure the purchase in this way. However, it may not be the most sensible way to proceed and you should consult your lawyer.

Developers have different policies when it comes to defining the plans and specifications for off-plan detached properties. Most developers offer a choice of models (to predefined plans and specifications) but limit the changes buyers can make to superficial issues, such as colour schemes or pre-installed kitchen equipment. Developers are reluctant to allow more substantial changes as these increase the complexity and costs. Some, however, will offer the option of working with their architects to draw up plans from scratch, which will be more costly but may be the only way to realize a unique property vision.

Self-build

A variation of buying off-plan is to build your own property, where you take on the roles of developer and client. This enables you to build your dream property to your exact tastes and specifications whilst avoiding paying a developer's margin, although developers' costs may be lower, which mitigates your potential savings. However, if you wouldn't consider building a property at home in the UK then all the more reason not to consider it in Spain. A self-build project is quite complex, so consider this option only if you have the time, willpower, know-how, resources and character to make a success of it.

Newly-built properties

Due to constant improvements in regulations, materials and building practices, a newly-built property from a good developer is an attractive option that appeals to over 30 per cent of British buyers. If you want a new property but do not fancy waiting for it to be built, or would prefer to avoid the uncertainties inherent in buying off-plan, then a newly-built property is the obvious choice.

There has never been a better time to buy newly-built properties on the Spanish coasts. Both developers and investors are trying to sell in a market where there are too many properties chasing too few buyers, which gives buyers more choice and negotiating power. In this market, buyers who take their time and do their research may be able to pick up bargains.

Another advantage of buying a new property is the relative simplicity of the purchase. Because it is brand new, you do not have to get involved in any refurbishments, which are often required with resales (see below). However, you would be well advised to have a professional snagging check done on a new property before buying (see page 157), and you should try to ensure that the vendor pays for any problems to be corrected.

Resale properties

Many British buyers are more interested in resales, or previously-owned properties (*segunda mano*), than newly-built ones (*nueva construcción*). Fortunately for them, the resale market is much bigger than the one for new property, and offers greater variety. However, properties that have been lived in suffer from wear and tear, so resales often need some degree of refurbishment after purchase. This may range from nothing more than a lick of paint and some minor repairs or a new kitchen and bathroom to a major modernization or restoration project. Only 10 per cent of British buyers claim that they are prepared to take on major renovations, which suggests that their expectations are on the low side concerning the extent to which refurbishments are necessary. However, about 40 per cent say they are prepared to undertake minor work, such as re-plastering and re-painting, which can be done quickly and cheaply without much risk of costs spiralling out of control or long delays in progress.

Location and surroundings

Along with the type and physical state of the property you want to buy, you also have to consider the location and surroundings that will suit you. Although you cannot be expected to visit every region in Spain before purchasing, it is important to do some research before focusing your search on a specific region.

Surroundings

You may have an overriding reason, such as family members or friends who are already living there, to choose a particular area of Spain, but you have a bigger choice than most people realize, and different surroundings suit different needs. Choosing the right area for you will go a long way towards ensuring that your property purchase is a success.

In the past, most British buyers opted for properties on coastal housing developments. However, tastes are changing, and now only 35 to 40 per cent say they intend to buy on a residential development or gated community, including golf developments. In reality, the majority will always end up buying on residential developments due to the choice, convenience, security and community they offer. Nonetheless, the buying intentions of the British in Spain are less homogeneous than they used to be, and the market is evolving to meet new types of demand. Approximately 50 per cent of British buyers now consider buying in a rural or village environment, whilst five to 10 per cent are opting for Spanish city life.

Urbanizations

In English, the term 'housing developments' does not sound particularly attractive, but in Spain, where they are known locally as urbanizations (*urbanización*), they are popular with affluent Spaniards as well as overseas buyers, and are home to the vast majority of the country's detached new properties. The variety of urbanizations is increasing as the market evolves, with more targeted at specific niches and offering a wider choice of semi-detached properties and apartments. Indeed, anyone who wishes to buy off-plan or a newly-built property is likely to end up buying on an urbanization.

Benefits

There are different types of urbanizations, ranging from simple estates with basic infrastructure (roads, street lighting, utility delivery and sewage) to luxury gated developments with an impressive range of services and facilities which often include a golf course. Common to them all are the municipal regulations that determine the estate's infrastructure, distribution and build-density. Urbanizations will also have a *comunidad de propietarios* – or community of owners – to which all the owners belong and contribute financially, which is responsible for

Villas on many new urbanizations are built close together.

managing the services and zones that are of mutual benefit. In general, this means that urbanizations offer greater convenience and security for property owners. Developers of some urbanizations only install the basic infrastructure and then sell off plots to individuals who wish to build their own properties. At the other extreme are the developers who provide a full building service. Generally speaking, Spain's golf developments, which are also urbanizations, provide the most complete service, including, in many cases, property management.

Location

Urbanizations are a relatively recent phenomenon, and they have proved to be very popular with Spain's increasingly affluent middle classes. They have mushroomed around cities like Madrid and Barcelona, creating dormitory suburbs. They have also spread rapidly along Spain's coastline, and in the space of 50 years the coastal areas have gone from being some of Spain's cheapest and most pristine land into one long semi-urban strip which is characterized by relatively high land and property prices.

Foreign buyers have always focused on the coastal urbanizations due to the attractions of the beach, sea views and the climate, and in some areas communities have been created consisting almost entirely of British and Irish owners. German and Scandinavian enclaves also exist, although mixed developments are increasingly common. When visiting an urbanization it is usually easy to get a feel for its community profile, and the developer's sales material and staff also provide obvious clues.

Urbanizations that appeal to foreign buyers are now starting to emerge further inland, often within 45 minutes' drive-time of the coast. Inland urbanizations tend to be cheaper than their counterparts on the coast, and also benefit from the more tranquil environment of the countryside. Many target niche markets, such as retirees, and this trend of inland urbanizations that appeal to specific buyer segments is set to continue.

They do offer a convenient solution for foreign buyers and thus will always have the lion's share of the market, but if you are looking for a permanent or semi-permanent home rather than a holiday home, be aware that many urbanizations on the coast effectively close down from

October to May and only come alive during the crush of the summer peak season. Some buyers are surprised that for most of the year there is nobody there – no neighbours, closed shops and restaurants – unlike July and August when the places are swamped with Spanish and other EU nationalities with their families. You really need to visit urbanizations out of season to identify which of them sustain life throughout the year. The one you buy on should be chosen to fit in with the way you plan to use the property.

The La Manga Club urbanization in Murcia is a very good example of a well-planned development that offers buyers a range of facilities all the year round.

3 Types of property

Urban or rural?

As we have seen, housing developments offer a suburban living environment, but most of them are on the built-up coasts or clustered around cities and towns and few have 'high street' amenities on site, with the exception of the macro-developments. If you want to be surrounded by a full range of amenities, then you should consider buying in one of Spain's towns or cities.

People who prefer city life to suburban or rural living will find themselves spoilt for choice in Spain. Barcelona, Madrid, Palma de Mallorca, Valencia, Alicante, Malaga, Seville, Cadiz, Santiago de Compostela, Ibiza and Granada are just a few of the many cities that are attractive if you are looking for a vibrant urban setting for a new life in the sun. Some of the smaller towns, such as Antequera in Andalusia or Zafra in Extremadura, are also emerging as popular destinations for buyers.

Even greater numbers of foreign buyers have started house-hunting in Spain's rural interior. Given the need for easy access to an international airport and the better climate in the coastal regions, this trend is still limited to an area which is no more than 100 kilometres inland from the coast. Rural living will not suit everyone, however, and people tend to take poor decisions based on romantic dreams of the rural idyll rather than first-hand experience of the reality. You need to be honest with yourself, do some hard thinking and, best of all, rent for six months in a rural area before buying.

'Land grab' law

For people considering buying rural property in the Valencian region a word needs to be said about what has come to be known as the 'land grab' law. Known in Spain as the *Ley Reguladora de la Actividad Urbanìstica* (LRAU), this law was introduced to facilitate the process of urban development in areas that have always been zoned for development. The original law was poorly drafted in key respects that gave promoters an unfair advantage by allowing them to develop land against the wishes of local property owners, in some cases forcing the owners to contribute to the development costs. The Government of the Valencian Region has passed a revised law that will make it easier for local property owners to block development proposals that affect their properties, and to present their own proposals. The original law, although undoubtedly poorly drafted, has been largely exaggerated and misreported in the British press. Even so, you should always consult your lawyer on this issue when buying in what appear to be rural areas of the Valencian region.

On the coast

There are a few points to bear in mind if your heart is set on the coast. As a general rule, the closer to the coast you go the higher the prices. Sea views are much sought after and command a premium, as do properties that are within walking distance of a beach.

Life on the coast can challenge your patience in July and August, when the whole world seems to descend upon the thin sliver of the beach near your home. Roads can turn into one long traffic jam and booking a table in a restaurant becomes a Herculean task. If, like most of the Spanish, you are a beach-fanatic, then easy access to the beach will be non-negotiable, but owning a property near the coast with access to a garden and pool is a compromise whereby you can still enjoy the climate and surroundings without having to fight your way to the beach. If easy beach access is not a key requirement, think twice about paying the premium for being close.

want to know more?

Take it to the next level...

► **Researching Spanish property** 54
► **Defining your needs** 58
► **Arranging property visits** 78

Other sources...
► **The Royal Institute of Chartered Surveyors has advice on property in Spain on their website: www.rics.org**
► **For more information on types of property, buy** *Spanish Homes Magazine*, **a monthly magazine available at newsstands in the UK.**
► **To weigh up the pros and cons of different types of property, see: www.spanishpropertyinsight.com/property.htm**

4 Researching the market

Many people rush from the first impulse to buy a home in Spain to signing a purchase contract for a property. Although this might result in a happy ending, the probability is high that it will lead to problems and regrets. It is much better to take your time and go about realizing your 'dream' in a more structured way. In this chapter, we look at sensible ways to approach the challenge of buying a Spanish property.

Doing the research

When you consider how expensive purchasing a property is, it is amazing how little research many people do before buying one in a foreign country. Background research is always time well spent and those who make the effort to do so will significantly increase their chances of making a successful purchase.

Background

People who buy in a hurry without doing enough research are more likely to pay too much and walk into the usual pitfalls with their eyes shut. It is a good idea to start your research as early as possible and certainly before you visit Spain to view some potential properties. Your research should continue throughout the time that you are looking to buy, although the focus will gradually shift from general background research to investigating specific issues.

Background research is not a challenge that can be solved like a mathematical equation – there is no correct answer to prove and all you can do is try to get as clear an idea as possible of the issues you face. Information empowers us to make more rational and objective decisions, whereas decision-making in the dark is a risky business.

Objectives

Broadly speaking, your objectives throughout this period of valuable background research should be as outlined below:
▶ To clarify the areas you wish to focus on.
▶ To get a feel for the property market in the areas that interest you.

- ▶ To identify the specific types of property that are best suited to your particular needs and budget.
- ▶ To get a reasonable idea of what life is like in those areas (especially during the periods when you plan to use the property).
- ▶ To identify any major risk factors when buying in Spain in general and in those areas in particular.
- ▶ To identify individuals and companies that you might consider dealing with during your purchase.
- ▶ To help prepare a clear, written brief.

The methods you can use to achieve these objectives should include a blend of the following – all of them, if possible.

Visiting Spain

In the course of doing your research, there is no substitute for visiting Spain under your own steam and spending time in the areas you are considering. Once again, this might seem like a statement of the obvious but it is surprising how few people do this. Holidays are one way to get a feel for an area but they are not ideal and should not be used as the only basis for your research. They tend to present too many distractions and may give you a distorted impression of an area, especially if you are planning to buy a permanent or semi-permanent home. Therefore you should set aside some time for a dedicated visit with the specific intention of learning about the local property market and community. In an age of low-cost travel the cost and effort of doing this is a small price to pay when you consider the size of the investment you are going to make.

The ideal way to research is to rent in the area for a few months before buying. If everyone were to do this there would be far fewer problems and regrets than is the case. However, this is often not practical, especially for people who are still working, in which case a week-long 'intelligence gathering' visit is much better than no visit at all.

The right attitude
It is very important that you do your background research in the right frame of mind. You are trying to build up a picture that will help you take the right decision when the time comes. Consider setting yourself a time frame but don't rush it. Start a file in which you keep all your notes and findings and try to be organized about the way you proceed. Do avoid any contact with pushy salesmen in this period as they have remarkable powers of persuasion and their input is not helpful.

Intelligence gathering

The purpose of your visit should be to gather as much information as possible on property and life in the area (at different times of the year). Visit under your own steam so that you are completely free to decide what you look at and whom you talk to. If a company is paying for or subsidising your visit you will not have this freedom and will probably only see and hear what suits them. During your visit you should drive around visiting as many urbanizations, developments and residential areas as possible. Don't be shy about talking to expats – they are easy to spot and are usually more than happy to chat to you. Talk to rental companies in the area if rental potential is an important requirement of yours; they know their business and are more likely to tell you the truth about the rental market than estate agents trying to make a sale. By all means look in estate agents' windows and visit properties to get first-hand experience of what is on the market. However, if you are just researching, never lose sight of the purpose of your visit and try to avoid rushing into a purchase in a bout of over-enthusiasm.

Internet research

The internet is a fantastic tool for doing background research. With a few clicks you can find information on any part of Spain and the property market in most areas. As well as looking for information on properties you should try to identify if there are any common problems affecting a specific area. This can be done by using well chosen search terms with combinations of words that might flush out the problems, and by looking beyond the first couple of pages of search results.

Online forums are also a useful source of information that often reveal common problems and allow you to make contact with other buyers, owners and residents in different regions. Expat community websites for specific areas are another rich source of information that you should look into.

Press

In recent years hardly a day goes by without an article on buying property or living in Spain appearing in the UK national and regional press. Although many of these articles tend to focus on the 'dream' of owning a Spanish property, they can also be a useful source of information on the common problems that people encounter when they are buying a home in Spain.

Exhibitions

Quite a number of overseas property exhibitions are held throughout the year around the UK. Many of them are organized by independent exhibition companies and bring together a range of different exhibitors, often from various countries. These types of shows are normally staged in one of the big regional exhibition centres, such as the NEC in Birmingham, or Olympia or Earls Court in London. Look out for advertisements in the national press or search the internet for details of the big exhibitions around the UK. Spanish estate agents and developers also organize their own private exhibitions but on a much smaller scale. These are held over a weekend, usually in a local hotel, and will be promoted in the local press. In this case there is only one exhibitor, although estate agents often invite a selection of developers to accompany them.

In the course of your background research, it is worthwhile visiting some exhibitions as they allow you to get a feel for the types of companies and individuals selling Spanish property, as well as collecting information on different regions. However, be aware that most companies will try and sign you up on the spot for a visit if you talk to them, and they can be surprisingly persuasive. Many of the 'inspection visits' on offer are free or heavily subsidised and seem like a cheap and easy way to research the market in an area, but they have also been carefully designed to close sales rather than inform people of their options. Inspection trips are not a good way to research the market and should only be considered once you are confident about the type of property you want, the area you want to buy in, and the company you want to buy from. So when visiting overseas property exhibitions whilst you are doing background research don't allow yourself to be persuaded into committing yourself to a visit you are not ready for.

Defining your needs

Once you feel that you have gone far enough in achieving the research objectives set out at the beginning of this chapter, you can move on to defining your needs, selecting companies and arranging to visit properties with a view to buying.

Clarify your ideas

Buying a Spanish property should not be approached frivolously. It is a big investment in time and money, and the result is likely to have a significant impact on your life, so you need to think hard about why you want to own a home in Spain and what you should buy given your circumstances. This helps you to clarify your ideas and enables you to do sufficient research. Many people allow their dreams and wishful thinking to cloud their judgement; if they fail to do the hard thinking at the start, they are more likely to waste their time and be disappointed.

Work out what you need

Once you have done some background research into the market the next step towards a successful purchase lies in analyzing and defining your needs. Doing so will not only help you to understand and prioritize your requirements but will also enable you to prepare a clear, written brief which describes the characteristics of the property you need. This useful document will help guide your search; you can share it with estate agents and other professionals so they don't waste time showing you unsuitable properties. Wishful thinking does more harm than good, so pay heed to the following advice.

▶ Be dispassionate and realistic when you are defining your requirements for a property.

▶ Think very hard about your circumstances both now and in the future.

▶ Identify the property characteristics that will fit in best with your evolving circumstances.

▶ Challenge your own assumptions about what you really want and need.

Be honest with yourself during this process, even though it may involve shooting down a few fantasies. For example, a rural property can be very appealing but the isolation often ruins the idyll for some people. You need to identify the important issues at the outset rather than once you have bought, and be sure to include everyone who is affected by the decision and arrive at a consensus that they can all support. It is a recipe for disaster if your children or partner are not fully supportive.

In the process of working out exactly what you need from a property in Spain, it is always helpful to talk to people you know who already own a place there. You can learn from their experience when it comes to deciding what and where to buy.

Do you want a villa with sea views and which is within easy walking distance of a beach and shops? Work out in advance exactly what you need from a property.

Questions to consider

Needs are as varied as the individuals who have them so it would be impossible to create a complete list of issues to consider. However, here are some of the questions most commonly asked; they need careful consideration.

What do your family need?

Take into account what they require. For example, if you have young or teenage children, your life will be a lot easier if you buy a property that allows them to have fun without you having to drive them everywhere.

What sized property do you need?

Be realistic about the size of property you need. Do not buy one on the assumption that extended family will always be staying, as you may end up with something that is too big for you. Focus on your own requirements.

What kind of property do you need?

Different kinds of property – new build or resale, villa or apartment, on-estate or off-estate – suit different needs, and it is important that you are aware of their relative merits before deciding what to buy. This is one of the most important questions that you need to answer.

How much effort do you want to put into maintenance?

The bigger the house and garden, the more time and money you will have to dedicate to looking after them.

Which region best suits your needs?

Different regions suit different needs, so be clear about what each one has to offer. If you are attracted to a region because of family and friends who are already living there, then the decision is more straightforward.

How important is accessibility?

Convenient access will be important to you if you wish to travel regularly. As an expatriate you will probably find that you need good access, both for you and for the convenience of family and friends who may wish to visit.

What is important in terms of surroundings?

Some properties offer rural charm; others offer urban glamour. Being in the centre of town, right on the beach or out in the countryside has advantages and disadvantages. What you choose will depend on which qualities you value the most at this time of your life.

What kind of community do you need?

This is particularly important if you are relocating to Spain. You will need an adequate social life to enjoy living there.

What level of security do you need?

Holiday homes make for easy targets, so if you are buying a property that will stand empty for most of the year, look for extra security measures, such as a gated urbanization.

Is investment a primary or secondary concern?

If you are buying as an investment, focus on the type of property that will yield the greatest potential in these terms.

Drawing up a clear brief

Draw up a written brief describing the characteristics of the property you want. It has to be realistic in terms of your financial resources. The act of writing it will help clarify your thoughts and articulate your priorities. It's a useful document for managing your search and letting estate agents know what you want, and will make it more difficult for them to ignore your requirements and waste your time. Although it helps to have a written brief before you start contacting agents, it should not be set in stone. Searching for property in Spain is a learning process and you may need to update your brief in the light of experience. It will evolve to adapt to the reality of the market, and the process of updating it will help you to manage your search.

want to know more?

Take it to the next level...

▶ **Spanish property prices** 10
▶ **Cost of buying** 160
▶ **Cost of owning** 166

Other sources...

▶ **For more on property exhibitions in the UK: www.internationalprop ertyshow.com**
▶ **An online forum to learn from other buyers and owners of Spanish properties can be accessed at: www.spanishpropertyin sight.com/forums**
▶ **The Foundation Institute of Foreign Property Owners was set up to help buyers and owners. Go to: www.fipe.org**

5 Getting ready to buy

Before buying a property in Spain you will need to make certain arrangements, such as opening a bank account and finding a lawyer. If you are serious about buying, it is a good idea to get these things in hand at the very start of your property search. If you leave them until you find a suitable property you will have to act under pressure and are more likely to make poor decisions and incur higher costs. Ideally, you need to have everything in place so that when you find the right property you are ready to move with speed, not haste.

Be prepared

The arrangements that you make will depend on your individual needs and circumstances, but here is some general advice and useful guidelines on the sort of measures you should explore and put into place before starting your search in earnest.

must know

Genuine lawyer
Make sure you use a genuine, qualified Spanish lawyer. If necessary, ask to see their diploma of qualification.

Finding an independent lawyer

It is important that you find your own, independent lawyer (*abogado*) rather than using one recommended by your estate agent or developer (see page 26). You need a lawyer you can trust on hand to check the very first contract you are expected to sign, which means looking for someone to act on your behalf before you have found the property you want to buy – ideally, before you even contact estate agents or developers. The reason why you should not sign or pay a deposit without first checking with your lawyer is explained in a subsequent chapter on the conveyancing process (see page 110).

At this stage, you do not need to hire a lawyer and make any payments, as there is always a chance that your property search will come to nothing. All you need to do is to find a good lawyer whom you can contact the moment you find a property that you would like to buy.

You should also find out how much they charge and what services are included in the fee. Many lawyers charge around one per cent plus VAT of the value of the property you buy, whilst others charge by the hour or a flat fee irrespective of the property's value. Some lawyers include a post-purchase service, such as paying the transaction taxes and inscribing your title in the property register whilst others charge extra for this. If these services are not included in the fee then you should consider using a *gestor* (administrative professional), as they are usually cheaper than qualified lawyers.

Defining an ownership structure

There are various options to choose from when deciding how to structure the ownership of a property in Spain appropriately:

▶ Sole ownership
▶ Joint ownership
▶ Spanish company
▶ UK company
▶ Offshore company

Each of these options will have different fiscal and inheritance implications, and different running costs. This is a complicated matter which needs specialist advice to be properly understood. Most British people buy the simple way, which is in their own names, or shared with a spouse, and, in most cases, this is a sensible option. However, if you have any inheritance concerns - for example, you have remarried and want your partner, rather than your children, to inherit the property on your death – you need to consider one of the other options. Always discuss your needs and circumstances in the context of Spanish inheritance laws with your lawyer before deciding how to structure the purchase.

Getting specialist advice

If you are going to buy a small and inexpensive property then it is probably not worth your while going to great lengths to optimize the fiscal impact of your purchase. However, the more expensive the property, the more you will have to gain from spending money on specialist advice in order to reduce your tax exposure. High net worth individuals with complex financial arrangements and large budgets will need to use lawyers who specialize in cross-border tax efficiency. Most British buyers, with a budget of 200,000 euros or under, may not benefit much from getting advice from such specialist lawyers, but if you have children, depending on your age and circumstances, it is usually worth discussing the issue of Spanish inheritance tax and how to minimize it with your lawyer in Spain.

Buying through a company

If you decide that your interests are best served by buying through a Spanish limited company then you will need to make arrangements well in advance of buying the property. Off the shelf companies can be bought in Spain, but, in general, the process of setting up a company takes longer and is more expensive than in the UK. If you are going to buy through a Spanish company, then you will need to hire your lawyer at this stage to help you set it up. Bear in mind that tax laws in the UK are going through a period of change and may end up penalizing UK residents who own property in Spain through a company. If you are tax-resident in the UK, you should always consult your financial advisor before deciding how to structure your purchase in Spain. If you are or will be tax-resident in Spain, then you should also consult your lawyer. If you are wealthy and have, or will have, significant assets in both Spain and the UK, then you will need to consult a cross-border tax specialist.

Opening a bank account

You are certain to need an account with a local bank branch in Spain in order to make many of the usual payments that are part and parcel of owning property there. It is highly likely that you will also need a Spanish bank account in order to buy a property. This is because many private vendors will only accept a bank-guaranteed cheque drawn from an account in Spain. Developers selling new properties are also starting to insist on payments being made from a local bank account as recent laws on money-laundering make accepting payments from other countries more complicated. Therefore you would be well advised to open a bank account in Spain well ahead of your purchase of a property.

If you use a mortgage in Spain to finance your purchase, it often makes sense to open an account with the bank that lends you the mortgage. In this case, your choice of bank will be determined by the mortgage conditions that you are offered. However, if you do not take out a mortgage with a local bank, you will need to do some research on the retail banking conditions being offered by different banks.

Retail banking services and charges vary significantly and it is important to look into these issues before opening an account and buying a property. Pay particular attention to the fees that different banks charge for receiving transfers from abroad and for issuing bank-guaranteed cheques, both of which can add thousands of euros to the cost of your purchase if you

The imposing church in the centre of Lorca in Murcia. Living in the middle of a town can be beneficial as shops, banks and restaurants will all be easily accessible.

are not careful. To avoid a nasty shock, you will need to negotiate these fees in advance with the branch where you open your account.

Pre-arranging a mortgage

Most people need a mortgage (*hipoteca*) to help finance the purchase of their property, but even those who can afford to buy without one may benefit from taking one out. The question of how to evaluate and arrange a mortgage for a Spanish property is dealt with in the chapter on financial matters (see page 176) but you need to make your mortgage arrangements in advance so that you are in a position to move with speed but without haste when you find a property you want to buy. People who are forced to apply for a mortgage in a hurry will not have time to shop around and find the best mortgage conditions. Unfortunately, this makes them more likely to end up with an expensive and inflexible arrangement, which can add thousands of euros to the cost of their property over the lifetime of the mortgage.

So do your research and shop around now with a view to choosing a mortgage broker or lender and arranging the basic conditions of the mortgage by the time you have found your ideal property. This will put you in a stronger position if buying from a developer whose mortgage you have the option of taking over. Having researched mortgages in advance, you will be better placed to evaluate what is on offer before deciding whether or not to take it. It will also help you establish roughly how much you will be able to borrow.

A villa with its own pool basking in the hot sunshine is most people's dream home in Spain.

Foreign exchange trading accounts

Spain is part of the euro-zone, which means that you will need euros to buy a property there. The amount will depend upon the value of the property and the size of the euro mortgage, if any, that you use. Basically, you will need euros to pay for all the costs (property and transaction costs) that your euro-mortgage does not cover.

If you already have your funds in euros then you will not need to buy them, but most British buyers hold their own funds in pounds sterling, which means purchasing euros before they can proceed with buying their property. Generally, the most expensive way to buy euros is from your high street bank, while the cheapest way is from a specialist currency broker. Depending upon who you buy them from, the difference in price for the same amount of euros on the same day can add up to many thousands of pounds!

To buy euros at a competitive rate you will need to set up a trading account with one of the specialist currency brokers. This can usually be done quickly, so it is not necessarily an expensive mistake to leave it until you have found a property. However, exchange rate movements can be quite dramatic in relatively short periods of time, so it is sensible to discuss the exchange rate outlook with a specialist when you decide to buy and start fixing your budget. If it looks like the euro is on a strengthening trend (getting more expensive), it may make sense to buy euros many months before purchasing a property. If you place the right bet on exchange rate movements, you can save yourself thousands of pounds – or increase your budget significantly. However, nobody knows for sure what will happen to exchange rates in the future, not even the specialist brokers, so there are no guarantees that you will make the right decision. Nevertheless you should look into this issue, select a currency broker and open a trading account at this stage rather than in a rush later.

Requesting a foreigner identity number

All foreigners who are resident or own property in Spain or, for some other reason, pay taxes in Spain have to have an NIE number from the Spanish government. NIE stands for *número de identidad de extranjero* (foreigner identity number).

It used to be possible to buy a property and to pay the associated taxes on the basis of your passport number but this is now almost impossible. You need to request and receive an NIE number by the time you purchase a property in Spain. Getting an NIE number can take anything from two to six weeks, depending upon where you apply and how quickly the Spanish authorities deal with your application.

Find an insurance broker

If you take out a mortgage in Spain you may find that you need insurance as specified by your mortgage lender. Even if this is not the case, or you do not use a mortgage, you will still have to make your own arrangements to insure your property.

There are many English-speaking insurance brokers operating in Spain (as well as brokers in the UK offering insurance for property there) and you are unlikely to have any difficulty arranging insurance. Ideally, insurance cover should start the moment you take possession of your property, but in many cases you will not be able to get a binding quote until a couple of weeks before the policy is due to start. However, you should look into the question of insurance and try to find a good broker when you start house-hunting in Spain. This makes it easier for you to get the best quote with the least hassle when the time comes.

want to know more?

Take it to the next level...

▶ **Lawyers and mortgage brokers** 26
▶ **Selecting estate agents** 74
▶ **Arranging property visits** 78

Other sources...

▶ **The regional offices of the British Consulates in Spain can provide contact details of local professionals such as lawyers.**
▶ **For instructions and forms for obtaining NIE numbers, contact the Spanish Government's Department of Immigration on: http://extranjeros. mtas.es.**
▶ **Information on real estate lawyers, mortgage brokers, banking solutions and obtaining NIE numbers is supplied by: www.spanishpropertyin sight.com/solutions.htm**

6 House-hunting in Spain

Now that you have completed your dedicated research and preparation, the time has come to go to Spain and start looking for the property that is going to fulfil your needs and dreams. Everything you have done previously has been in preparation for this moment, and now the risks of making a wrong move increase. So don't get carried away and opt for something which is entirely unsuitable during your visit, as many people have done. Stick to your plan and look for the property that best fits your carefully researched brief.

Arranging property visits

The best idea is to rent in an area for several months and use the time to view properties with a selection of local agents. This will give you a feel for the area and the market, increases the number of properties you can view, and removes the pressure to make a quick decision that people on flying visits often have to make.

Types of visit

Many people cannot afford the luxury of renting in Spain before buying and have to make do with quick reconnaissance visits. In this case, it is important to plan each and every visit carefully (you may need to make several visits before you find the right property) to ensure that your time is well spent. If you exclude holidays, which are less than ideal for house-hunting, then there are two basic formats for visiting Spain to view properties. One is to liaise with estate agents but plan and finance the trip yourself, and the other is to go on a subsidised 'inspection trip' that many companies offer.

Inspection trips

Many of the biggest estate agencies and direct-sale developers offer inspection trips of three to four days' duration, which are either free or heavily subsidised. Clients are flown to Spain and are put up in a pleasant hotel at the company's expense, then herded around new developments in groups of buyers with similar budgets. During the first two or three days, they will be shown two or more 'projects' every morning and afternoon, and on the final day they will be expected to indicate which ones they would like to revisit. The aim of the inspection trip is to get the client to pay a reserve deposit before returning home.

The trips are sold as an easy and cheap way to view Spanish property. In theory, clients only have to indicate their budget and property preferences and then pick a convenient time to visit, rather like booking a package holiday. Everything is then arranged for them and the company picks up the bill.

However, there is no such thing as a free lunch and inspection trips are no different. If the company is paying for your trip it is only because it is in their interests to do so, not yours. They have complete control over the visit and decide exactly what you see and learn. Clients are wined and dined and told wonderful things about the properties they are shown but have no way of checking this information with other sources, or comparing these properties with the wider market. Inspection trips are also the perfect environment for applying pressure-selling techniques, and can be used to make clients feel obliged to the company that is paying for the trip. Many clients report

Properties that are built out of local stone are popular with both Spanish and foreign buyers.

that the royal treatment they receive at the start of a trip quickly evaporates if they subsequently decide not to buy.

On balance, inspection trips are better for the companies that offer them than the clients who go on them. They put the company in control and the client in the dark, and make it more likely that clients will overpay for mediocre properties. In this day and age of low-cost travel and the internet, inspection trips are a classic false economy for buyers.

Self-arranged visits

The best way to view properties is to arrange the visit yourself. You decide the dates, book your own flights, hotel and car, and liaise with the estate agents and developers you have chosen to deal with to organize property visits. This leaves you in command of the visit and prevents any one company from limiting your

The imposing façade of a country house in Catalonia in north-eastern Spain.

access to information. There is also no better way of ensuring that you see the widest selection of properties. Low-cost airlines and internet sites for booking hotels and cars have made it easier and cheaper to arrange your own visit than ever before.

Duration of visits

Three- or four-day visits are unlikely to give you sufficient time to view enough properties and initiate proceedings if you find one that you want to buy. One of the common reasons why people run into problems is because they rush into signing a reservation contract just before heading back to the airport to catch their flight home. Try to set aside a minimum of a week for a visit, which gives you time to visit a reasonable number of properties with several different companies, as well as spending time on other tasks such as talking to your lawyer or bank manager or simply exploring the area, which is always time well spent.

Planning visits

Plan your visits carefully and have a shortlist of properties or new developments to view based on the particulars and brochures you have been sent in advance. You can be flexible as new properties may come onto the market and your brief may change in the light of experience. However, if your time is scarce, focus on the properties most likely to suit you rather than try to see everything in your price range. By having detailed information and photos of the properties before you visit, you should be able to identify the ones worth looking at. However, photographs can be misleading, so if you have time, do try to visit some properties that might not have made your A-list.

If you have chosen to work with a buyer's agent or search and find consultant, you will need to coordinate your visit with them. Buyer's agents will have visited all the properties on your behalf, which means that you will only see the most suitable ones – a big advantage when your time is scarce.

Inspecting target properties

With a bit of luck you will see one or more properties that you could consider buying: target properties. When you identify these, the inspection becomes serious. You need to gather as much information as possible on them to help you make the right decision; if you find more than one, you will need this information to rank them in order of preference. It will also be useful in estimating how much money, if any, you will need to invest in refurbishing a property once you have bought it.

If you like the property based on the first walk around, and could see yourself living there, then it is a target. It is more than likely that you will be able to revisit, so this may not be your only chance to inspect it. However, work on the assumption that you may not have time, just to be on the safe side.

Do not confuse the information you gather during these visits with the legal and administrative checks – the due diligence – that need to be done when you move on to making an offer on a property and negotiating with the vendor. Those checks will be carried out by a lawyer, a surveyor or some other qualified professional. However, you can get much more information from your viewings than you might expect; it all depends upon how you go about it.

Because you need to inspect target properties in great detail, this can present problems for the estate agent and the vendor looking on. However, think about how much money you are being asked to pay and how much they will earn and then just get on with it, regardless of the looks you might attract. Make it clear that you are very serious about the property, so they will see your close inspection as less of a waste of time.

Carry out as many of the following checks as possible. Make notes on everything you observe, and do some quick sketches or take digital photos. Not all of the checks may be applicable, and some can be done after the visit as they do not require you to be physically present in the property.

Property structure and condition

Identify supporting walls and check their condition. Look for
serious cracks or other signs of distress in the main structural
features: supporting walls, beams, retaining walls, pool casing,
etc. Even an untrained eye should be able to tell the difference
between obvious structural faults and mere cosmetic problems,
such as hairline cracks in plastering. The trick is to identify and
scrutinize the structural elements. Simply knocking on a wall
with your knuckles is often enough to distinguish a dividing
wall from a supporting one. Structural problems are the most
complicated and expensive to resolve, so it is very important to
identify signs of them. Bulging walls are always a bad sign, as
are sagging roofs, which might indicate the need for major
building work, which can be very expensive.

On a hot, sunny day
most properties will
look attractive and
inviting but don't get
carried away. Make
sure the properties
you view and the one
you end up buying
fulfil your needs.

Subsidence

This does not seem to be much of a problem in Spain due to naturally low water tables and the dry climate, but you should still be aware of it. Subsidence is often caused by changing water content in clay soils, which causes the soil to swell and contract, thus undermining a property's foundations. This may be due to a falling water table or by trees and bushes absorbing water during an unusually dry spell. Subsidence can also be caused by water leaks that wash away the soil under the foundations of a property – when it has a high sand or gravel content. A professional survey will be required if you have any doubts about subsidence, and is a good idea in any event.

This is an obvious example of a Spanish villa with structural problems.

Leaking roofs

Pay attention to the roof. Is it pitched or flat? If it is pitched, what condition are the tiles in (or other surface materials)? If it is

flat, can you get onto it to check the waterproofing? Look for signs of a leaky roof both inside and outside the property.

Damp

This can affect newly-built properties as much as resales. Damp can rise from the soil through the foundations, or come through the walls, leaky roofs or other sources of poor drainage. If you see signs of damp, try to estimate the cause based upon its location in the property. It can always be treated with damp proofing, but this can be a big job.

Infestations

Look out for signs of infestations, such as woodworm in interior or exterior carpentry, or droppings from other pests. It can always be treated but it is better to know in advance.

Overall condition

You will need to form an opinion of a target property's overall condition. If you were to buy it, would you need to do any paintwork, plastering, wallpapering, flooring and tiling, joinery, draught proofing, insulation, exterior surfaces and weatherproofing? If you think you can live with the property 'as is', you will not have to spend any money on these issues. However, you may need to set aside a budget for cosmetic improvements.

Climate

The climate will determine the pressure the property is under from the elements, and whether you need central heating and air-conditioning. Properties in southern coastal areas (south of Valencia and including the Balearics and Canaries) benefit from a mild climate without the killer combination of water and frost. Properties in these areas do not need to be as sturdily built as in other regions, and even cheap, flimsy and badly built houses will usually survive. Even so, find out about local weather patterns – rainfall, sunshine, temperatures, humidity and wind – and consider how well the property's construction and features adapt to them. Some properties are better suited than others.

Parking

Pay particular attention to the car parking arrangements. For instance, if there is a private garage or carport how big is it and how secure? Is it adequate for your needs? Does it enjoy unimpeded access and would it be easy to manoeuvre in and out? If there is no private parking, how parked-up does the street appear, and does it look as if finding parking would be a problem? Unless you are buying an apartment in the centre of town you will probably need a car. The ease with which you can park, load and unload it will help to determine how convenient life is. Imagine returning from the supermarket with heavy bags of shopping, or from the airport loaded up with suitcases; how easy will those moments be given the parking arrangements of the property you are viewing?

Villas with private swimming pools are the most sought-after type of property.

Boundaries

When visiting a property it is important to walk the boundaries and see all the boundary points with your own eyes. Obviously this does not apply to apartments but it is essential if viewing properties with land, especially in rural areas. Boundaries are one of the biggest causes of disputes, and buyers often come away from a visit with a mistaken idea as to what is included. This may be because estate agents or vendors imply that the property is bigger than it actually is, or because they have not paid enough attention to identifying the boundaries.

So walk the boundaries if it is practical to do so, have the estate agent or vendor point out every boundary point, and take as many photos as are necessary. This will not only reduce any chance of misunderstanding but also make it more difficult for you to be misled if you proceed with purchasing the property. Interpreting the maps and deeds that make up the formal description will be much easier, especially in rural areas where they do not always match the land you were shown.

Furniture, fixtures and fittings

When visiting resale properties, find out what is included in the price. Some are offered for sale with some furniture included or fully furnished, whereas others will be stripped bare when the property is vacated. Clarify this, especially regarding kitchen and laundry equipment, white goods, interior furniture, shelving, lighting, mirrors, and garden and pool furniture and equipment. Anything you buy over and above the permanent fixtures should be clearly documented in an inventory that will form part of the purchase contract.

Surroundings

Find out about the immediate surroundings of any target property you visit as they can have a big impact on your quality of life if you decide to move there, whether it's on a temporary or permanent basis. You can do this research on your own after the visit; you don't need access to the property.

Proximity of facilities

Start off by identifying and plotting on a map the facilities in the area. This helps you to assess how much value the area has to offer and to compare the area value of one property with another. Although there will not be much difference between two properties on the same street, even ones a few kilometres apart can have a different area value. Find out where all the useful and desirable facilities are located - supermarkets, fresh food markets, health food shops, bakeries, newsagents, tobacconists, post office, restaurants, banks, hotels, gyms, cinemas, police stations, schools, hospitals or clinics, access roads and public transport points, not forgetting beaches and golf courses. Easy access to these facilities is a big asset to a property. Your individual needs will determine how much value you give to their proximity.

Physical risk factors

Think about the lie of the land and whether there could be hidden problems related to it. Some urbanizations have been built on the flood plains of rivers and are flooded every decade or so. Although these problems are quite rare, urbanizations affected by them are often marketed heavily to foreign buyers, who, unlike the locals, are unaware of them. Drive around the immediate area looking for physical features that might indicate a risk factor, e.g. flooding, fires or waste pollution. These are relatively minor risks but they can exist. The vendor is unlikely to mention them and estate agents may not even know about them, so it's up to you to do your own research.

Local building works

You should also be be aware of how any building in the area might affect you. Future construction can cause considerable disruption with noise, dust and heavy vehicle traffic, not to mention ruining your view. Drive around and try to identify any land where building work might disrupt life in the property you are considering buying. Generally, you would be subject to this only if building takes place within sight or hearing distance, but some urbanizations are used as an access road to big building projects further afield.

Local lifestyle

Try to get a general impression of the immediate area. Drive around at different times of the day. Get a feel for how noisy it is, especially at night. Explore the area within 15 minutes' drive of the property in all directions. Talk to local residents about living there. Everything you can find out is useful.

Explore the local area and see what if offers in terms of the facilities you need.

Community bylaws

If you are looking at a property on an urbanization or development, find out as much as you can about the community bylaws. If you decide to proceed with the purchase, what you discover may affect whether you make an offer. Ask the vendor or agent if there are any restrictions on the use of facilities, rentals, pets and so on.

end of your visit are your only guide as to what the finished property will be like. If the material is vague, then the chances are that you will end up with a property that is quite different to what you were expecting, usually for the worse. You should only consider buying on those developments where you are given sufficiently clear and detailed information.

The developer's reputation

The promoter's professionalism and approach to business will also play a big part in how successful your purchase turns out to be. You will rely on the developer to deliver what you are expecting in the time frame that is agreed, so their reputation is extremely important. It is a sad fact, however, that there are some poorly-run and unscrupulous promoters operating in Spain – both British and Spanish – whose only aim is to get as much money from the client in return for as little as possible.

Use your visit to find out whatever you can about the developer, although you only need to do this in depth if you decide to buy a property. Talk to some previous clients and do some internet searches using terms that include the developer's name, the development name, and key words like 'problems'.

Remember that every detail of contact you have with the developer, such as how the staff are presented and behave, the brochure quality and presentation, etc., reflects the way in which the organization is run. It does not matter whether the developer is big or small; what matters is their business philosophy and professionalism. Therefore it is important to try and establish this before you proceed to buy a property.

Golf is a big selling point for property in Spain. Ownership on or easy access to a golf course will help increase its value.

Show homes

If a show home is used, do clarify the relationship between its quality and the property you are being offered. Clients are often shown an exquisite show home, which is finished to a high standard, tastefully decorated and kitted out with the latest technology, but are disappointed when the property delivered bears no resemblance to it. Some developers are not trying to deceive their clients – just to impress them – but in the process their expectations are raised and thus disappointment is inevitable. However, some cynical developers intentionally mislead their clients by using show homes that are of a much higher quality than they intend to deliver. Therefore you must be sure to clarify how representative the show house is of the property that you are considering buying, and then confirm this by checking out the specifications you are given.

Payment terms

These should always be clear to potential buyers. Make sure you find out how much you are expected to pay, when the payments will become due, and what on-site build progress they will correspond to. An example of a common payment structure for an apartment purchased off-plan would be as below:

Apartment price: 300,000 euros plus VAT	
PAYMENT	**AMOUNT**
Reserve	3,000 euros
Private sale contract	25 per cent + VAT – reserve payment 75,000 + 5,250 – 3,000 = 77,250 euros.
Other stage payments	None
Final payment at signing of public deeds	75 per cent + VAT: 225,000 + 15,750 = 240,750 euros
Total payments	321,000 euros

Stage payment protection

Developers are obliged by Spanish law to insure your stage payments and to keep them in a separate account dedicated exclusively to building your property. This ensures that, should the developer fail before completing your property, you will not lose the money you have already paid. Although mandatory, there are some developers who do not comply with this law as it represents an extra financial burden for them. Clarify the stage payment protection arranged by the developer during your visit and get your lawyer to check this during due diligence. You should never buy off-plan from a developer who cannot demonstrate that your stage payments are guaranteed.

Apartment price: 300,000 euros plus VAT	
PAYMENT	AMOUNT
Reserve	3,000 – 6,000 euros (see page 148)
Private contract	20–30 per cent of the price (plus VAT @ 7 per cent and less the reserve payment already made).
Other stage payments	It depends upon the promoter and the type of property you are buying. Many promoters do not ask for any other payments beyond the initial one of, say, 25 per cent until completion, when the remaining 75 per cent plus VAT becomes due. Other promoters may ask for up to 50 or 75 per cent to be paid in stages while construction is in progress, with the remainder settled at the end.
Final payment	Whatever outstanding amounts (including VAT) are paid at the time of signing the public deeds of sale before Notary.

Mortgages

Many developers arrange a mortgage that you have the option of taking over. You are not obliged to do this, although doing so will probably save you some arrangement fees. However, this potential saving needs to be evaluated in terms of the overall

mortgage; saving a few hundred euros in arrangement
fees but then paying dearly over the rest of the
mortgage's lifetime is a raw deal. Compare the
developer's mortgage with other offers; to do this,
gather information on the mortgage during your
visit. You may be put under pressure to take over
the developer's mortgage, as they may have to pay
a cancellation fee if you don't.

Deadlines

During your visit, find out about delivery dates and penalties if these dates
are not met. These should be included in the private contract you will sign
if you proceed to buy. Ask the developer how you will be kept informed of
construction progress. This question may be met with a look of astonishment
but it is not difficult for them to email a monthly progress report (milestones
signed off by an architect) plus photos. The more demanding buyers become,
the quicker developers will have to improve to meet these demands.

Planning permission

Ask the developer to clarify the status of the planning permission for the project
you are visiting. Your lawyer will have to confirm this during the due diligence
but it helps if you clarify it at this stage. Many people have bought into projects
that don't have planning permission and often have come to regret it.

Example contracts

If you are seriously interested in a new development, ask for the example
contracts you will be expected to sign if you proceed. Your lawyer will check
these, along with other contractual documentation before you pay or sign
anything. The earlier you get this, the better. You will probably be expected
to sign two contracts when you buy a property off-plan from a developer:
a reserve contract to accompany the reserve payment, which is followed
about 30 days later by a private sale contract, and corresponding payments
you have agreed with the developer. Avoid signing the first of these contracts
on the spot when you visit, whatever pressure is applied.

Community profile

Before you buy on a new development it helps to have an idea of the community and social life it offers. Neighbours can make a significant contribution to your enjoyment of life there. Find out as much as you can about your fellow buyers - their nationality, age, family status - with a view to deciding whether this is the sort of community you are looking for. Establish also whether it is predominantly a holiday development which will be deserted out of season. If possible, talk to the other buyers on the development.

Security on new developments

New developments with a common security policy can offer better protection than other types of property. Ask what provisions will be made for security, if any – many developers leave this decision up to the community of owners once it has been established. A new development with a year-round residential community will offer you much better protection than a holiday development, for obvious reasons. The ideal solution, however, is a gated community with 24-hour security.

Services and facilities

Some new developments have a golf course, health and fitness club, clubhouse, hotel, shops and restaurants on site, whilst others have none at all. The more facilities you have access to, the greater your chances of enjoying the property and the easier it will be to sell one day. Social facilities create an environment for making new friends (important for people with children). Some developers make arrangements to help buyers with property management, such as house and garden cleaning, maintenance and rental. However, these kinds of services are provided usually only on larger developments.

want to know more?

Take it to the next level...

▶ **Where to look** 12
▶ **Types of property** 34
▶ **Making an offer** 120

Other sources...
▶ **For travelling to Spain you can find out which low-cost carriers fly to which Spanish airports:** www.flightmapping.com
▶ **For information on surveys in southern Spain, see:** www.surveyspain.com
▶ **For information on surveys in northern Spain, see:** www.blakemorewalker.com
▶ **For information on surveys in the Balearics:** www.propertyworksonline.com
▶ **For more information on house-hunting in Spain:** www.spanishpropertyinsight.com/househunting.com

7 Buying a previously-owned property

A previously-owned property is known in the trade as a resale property, and this is the first choice of many buyers. Once you identify a property you want to buy, the risks and benefits will become very real. If you get the purchase wrong you could lose a substantial amount of money and end up with something which is nothing but a burden to you. However, if you get it right, you will not only own a property that is likely to be a good investment but it will also enhance your happiness and quality of life.

Estate agents' commissions

Take these into consideration when formulating your negotiations strategy. Unlike UK agents who earn a percentage of the transaction price, Spanish vendors tend to present their agents with a non-negotiable net amount they want from the sale, and leave it to them to charge whatever commission they can get away with on top of this. Agents are likely to add on 10 per cent or more, hoping to end up with five per cent or more. Buyers may assume they are discussing the price with the vendor when in reality they are simply negotiating the size of the commission with the agent. Foreign vendors will probably agree a percentage fee of the final price with the agent (as they do at home), but if the vendor is Spanish, the agent may defend the highest price possible, as every euro above the vendor's net amount goes into their commission. Ask the agent which method is being used to determine the commission. Estate agents can even benefit from bringing the commission out into the open and negotiating it with you, although it might take an enlightened one to appreciate this.

Issues to negotiate

There are certain key issues which have to be negotiated with the vendor, and these are as follows:

The price and undeclared value

You will want to agree the lowest price possible. The undeclared value is the amount of the price (if any) to be paid 'under the table' and not declared in the deeds. Many Spanish vendors still ask for a percentage of the price in cash (referred to as 'B' or *negro*), but resist this if possible. It is a fiscal fraud that mainly benefits the vendor whilst the potential liabilities accrue to the buyer. It is still common in Spain, and sometimes it is impossible to buy a property without paying a percentage in this way. Five to ten per cent of the price may be manageable, but the more you pay, the greater the risk. Always try to avoid undeclared cash payments, especially if the property has sitting tenants.

Some developments tend to be very large and encompass all sorts of facilities, such as this one at La Manga. Prices on these developments are often high but they are a very good investment and easy to sell at a later date.

The deposit payment method

If you sign a private contract that involves you paying a deposit of, for instance, 10 per cent of the price, then you need to agreed a payment method that is acceptable to both you and the vendor. The options are as follows:

▶ Pay the funds to the vendor.

▶ Pay the funds to the estate agent.

▶ Pay the funds to the vendor's lawyer.

▶ Pay the funds to your lawyer.

Paying the funds direct to the vendor will suit them nicely, but if they were to back out of the sale this could make it more difficult for you to get your deposit back, so don't do it. It is better to pay the deposit to a third party, such as a lawyer (ideally yours), who can be expected to pass the deposit on to the appropriate party according to the contract and the outcome. In practice, it is common to pay the deposit to the estate agent, which is not a problem if they are professional and trustworthy. However, it is difficult to know which estate agents to trust and therefore, in most cases, you should avoid paying them a deposit.

Whichever third party you pay the deposit to, check if they have a bonded escrow account that provides extra protection for you. Unfortunately, few Spanish lawyers or estate agents have such accounts, so you may have to make do without this. Whichever method you agree with the vendor, make sure you have the necessary bank details to make the payment on time.

The negotiations process

This traditional-style villa is in a rural setting. An increasing number of buyers are now looking for cheaper country properties away from the noise and bustle of the coast.

This will vary from case to case but will usually be done via the estate agent, rather than directly with the vendor, and may take anything from a few days to several months. There is often an exasperating amount of going backwards and forwards with offer followed by counter offer, and just when you think you have reached an agreement some unforeseen problem is liable to crop up and throw everything into doubt. Prepare yourself for

Pre-emption rights and tenants

Your lawyer will need to find out if anyone has a pre-emption right over the property. This gives its holder a preferential right to buy the property at the price agreed between you and the vendor. This would be the case if there were sitting tenants with indefinite contracts. If you buy such a property, the sitting tenants will have the right to stay in it for the remainder of their rental contract. Unless you are specifically looking to buy such a property, avoid doing so. However, if you do proceed with the purchase, never agree to pay any of the price 'under the table' as there is a chance that the tenants could force you to sell them the property at the price declared in the deeds.

Debts, liens and embargoes

Although the contract you will sign should state that the property is sold free of any encumbrances, double-check this as the debts become yours once you own it. The land register will reveal any debts associated with it: a mortgage, loan, or unpaid taxes or penalties. These are not a problem if they are identified in advance and the vendors clear them before or at the time of signing the deeds. If the vendor has a mortgage on the property, this may be cancelled at the signing of the deeds (out of the money you pay to the vendor). You may be required to pay a cheque to the mortgage lender.

Payments of local taxes (IBI)

You also need to see the most recent receipts of payment of local rates (IBI) and, in some cases, check with the town hall (*ayuntamiento*) that there are no problems with unpaid rates from previous years. The town hall can issue a certificate to this effect. Unpaid rates become the new owner's liability.

The deeds

Your lawyer will need to check the existing deeds (*escritura*), so the vendor or estate agent must make a copy available to you. The deeds need to be checked to confirm that the property is correctly described in them before you proceed to buy. They contain descriptions of the amount of land (if any), boundaries, built areas, internal divisions, exterior recreational areas and other salient features.

Illegal or unregistered changes

Properties are often described inaccurately in the deeds for a number of reasons. The vendor or a previous owner may have carried out building work, such as an extension or a new pool, and not have registered these changes in the deeds. This may be because they were illegally carried out (without the town hall's permission) or because the owner forgot or could not be bothered with the time and expense of having the changes registered in front of a Notary.

In the latter case, the town hall will have a copy of the building work authorization (*licencia de obras* or *licencia de reformas*), as should the owner. If authorization from the town hall can be produced to justify the discrepancy between the physical reality of the property and the deeds, this can be used to update the deeds when you complete and sign before Notary. However, if the changes were carried out illegally, then the process becomes more complicated to resolve and you need to consult your lawyer as to the best way to have the changes legalized – if at all possible - before proceeding. Never buy a property with illegal features that are impossible to legalize.

This old country church in southern Catalonia has been converted into a residential property.

Misleading descriptions

Another reason why the property might appear to be incorrectly described in the deeds is because you have been misled as to what you are buying. This normally involves property with land, but it could also happen when buying on an urbanization, or any detached property. You must study the deeds and relate them to what you have been shown during the visit. This demonstrates why it is so important to take detailed notes and photos of a target property when you visit. You then need to have the deeds clearly explained to you by your lawyer, who should translate the relevant section so that you understand how the property is described. In an ideal world, your lawyer would be able to visit the property to confirm that it is as described in the deeds, so try and arrange this if possible.

Parking spaces

If you are buying a property that includes a private parking space then pay attention to how this is presented in the deeds. It might be in the same deed as the property, or in a separate deed, in which case it needs to be checked in the same way as the main

If you are buying a house or apartment in a town or round a marina, it is unlikely that you will get a car parking space.

Small villas located on urbanizations with a sea view are the most popular resale properties.

property. A separate deed is more complicated and means you have to pay separate taxes and slightly higher transaction charges, such as Notary fees, land register fees and stamp duty.

Resolving discrepancies

Do not buy a property until it is accurately described in the notarized title deeds, or another mechanism has been arranged by which you can be sure that accurate deeds can be notarized and inscribed in the property register. If there are illegal features that are not described in the existing deeds, negotiate an acceptable legalization process with the vendors. If necessary, consider agreeing to pay part of the costs of this process. Some discrepancies are too big or too illegal to sort out, however. If this is the case, and your lawyer will advise you, walk away. If you sign deeds before such things are resolved, the problem becomes yours alone.

Time restrictions

Some illegal features may become legal by virtue of the amount of time they have existed – normally after four years without any complaints from neighbours or orders from the town hall to remove them (*expediente de infración urbanística*). However, in this case you must have a registered architect certify that the feature is more than four years old (*certificado de antigüedad*) and get confirmation from the town hall before proceeding.

If you are viewing a property in an urbanized area, find out what is going to be built around it. Many people buy on the promise that nothing will ever be built to obstruct their view, only to find it is lost to an apartment block. Assume that if a five-storey apartment block can be built on the plot in front of the property that is what will happen. The urban plan (*plan urbanístico*) will reveal what can and cannot be built around the property you are considering.

Regional development plans

Check the overall development plans for the region with the town hall. These are contained in the general plan (*plan general*) and include plans for major projects, e.g. motorways, airports and railway lines. If you are buying in a consolidated urbanized environment, it is unlikely that you will be adversely affected by anything in the general plan. Outside of these areas, however, there is a very small chance that plans to build a motorway or reclassify rural land as development land could affect the property you are looking at.

The community of owners

If the property is part of a community of owners (*comunidad de propietarios*), as is nearly always the case for apartments and urbanizations, then you should check that the vendor is up to date with community fees (*gastos de comunidad* or *cuota de la comunidad de propietarios*). You also need to find out how much they are so you can budget for them, and check whether there are any plans afoot to upgrade the communal areas that might mean a large and unexpected cost shortly after you have purchased. You should also check the community bylaws for any that might affect you (such as restrictions on renting out properties). You can obtain all this information from the secretary or administrator of the community of owners (*administrador de la comunidad de propietarios*) who can also provide you with a copy of the community bylaws (*los estatutos de la comunidad de propietarios*).

Other issues

▶ Check the amount of *plusvalía* if the vendor is a non-resident, or if there is any chance that you might have to pay it.

▶ Obtain the exact postal address of the property.

▶ If the vendor is an off-shore company, confirm that the three per cent tax levied on this form of ownership has been paid to date.

▶ If the property is within 500 metres of the coast, confirm that it does not fall foul of the coastal planning law (*ley de costas*).

▶ If the property is being sold with furniture of any value, make sure you are provided with a signed inventory.

▶ Check that all utility bills are up to date by obtaining copies of the latest receipts from the vendor.

▶ Confirm you are not expected to pay the agent's commission.

▶ Find out if the vendor has technical plans and specifications for the property, and ask to see them. If the property is less than 10 years old, enquire into the builder's guarantee.

▶ On a rural property, check if any third parties have rights of way over the property, or whether you will need them over someone else's property. The same applies to water and hunting rights.

Communal facilities on a newly-built development. Check what will be put in before you buy.

Contracts

Once you have done all the checks that are appropriate in your case, and have been given the all clear by your lawyer, you can commit to buying a property by signing a private contract and paying a deposit.

This villa has a car port rather than garage parking. Be sure to check the parking arrangements before you sign any contracts if easy car access and parking are considerations.

Private contracts

In some cases you may be able to skip the private contract (*contrato privado de compraventa*) and go straight to signing the public deeds before Notary. This is possible if you are in a position to do the due diligence quickly and can move onto signing the public deeds in under a month. All the private contract does is buy you (or sometimes the vendor) time to

prepare for signing the deeds. If both you and the vendor can move quickly, there is no point in signing private contracts.

There are various private contracts you can sign before you get to the 'public' contract (the deeds you sign before a Notary). Private contracts are no less binding on the buyer and seller than the public deeds, but they cannot be inscribed in the land register without the Notary's signature, and they are not binding on third parties, such as the vendor's creditors.

Option contract (*contrato de opción de compra*)

With this contract you pay an agreed amount to the vendor and in return they commit to sell you the property at a fixed price if you exercise the option to buy within the agreed time frame. If you fail to do this, you lose the money you have paid for the option, and the vendor is no longer contractually obliged to sell you the property. That would be the end of the matter and you would have no grounds to dispute the contract in court.

Reservation contract (*documento de reserva*)

This requires you to pay a deposit to reserve a property for a specified period of time, usually 30 days. At the end of this period you either back out and lose your deposit or proceed to a more substantial contract that commits you to buying, such as a deposit contract, a private sale contract or even the public deeds. If you proceed, the vendor is contractually obliged to sell you the property at the agreed price. The deposit is usually between 3,000 and 6,000 euros and counts towards the final price of the property. British buyers will almost certainly be asked to sign a reservation contract when they are buying from a developer, and estate agents may also try to get them to sign up when buying resale property.

There is a good reason for this but not one that favours the buyer. Agents want to turn the momentum and enthusiasm of your visit into a commitment as quickly as possible. If you return home having signed a reservation contract and paid a non-refundable deposit of 6,000 euros, then you are more likely to proceed with the purchase than if you depart having seen a property that you plan to buy but without having made any commitment. The deposit makes a change of mind more costly.

to the Notary's escrow account if this is permitted. Your lawyer should inform the Notary of whichever payment method you agree with the vendor.

▶ Arrange a mortgage valuation - if you have been unable to arrange one by this stage, you must have one carried out now. You will not be granted a mortgage without a valuation, and this will determine how much you can borrow. You will also have to inform your mortgage lender of the date, time and place of the signing of deeds, as their representative has to be present.

▶ Withdraw cash if necessary - if you have agreed to pay a part of the price in cash you will have to withdraw it before you go to the Notary. Depending upon the amount, this can be quite a challenge. Be warned that there are restrictions on the amount of cash you can withdraw from your bank, even if you have the funds in your account. Always check in advance how much cash you can withdraw in one transaction without raising questions.

▶ Remind the vendor that a certificate from the president of the community of owners, if relevant, and signed by the president and the administrator, is required - you need to do this at least 10 days in advance of the signing. This certificate (*certificación sobre las deudas con la Comunidad de Propietarios*) will need to be shown to the Notary during the signing.

▶ Check which documents you need to bring to the signing - as a minimum, you will need your passport (or Spanish residency card if you have one) but you may also be required to produce an NIE number and other documents, e.g. birth and marriage certificates, or even official translations of these.

▶ Check the exact postal address of the property – this may not be the same as the address given in the deeds.

▶ Gather information for changing the utility contracts – this means getting copies of all the latest utility bills from the vendor. Make a note of the telephone number. If more than three months have passed since your lawyer checked that all local taxes and utility payments are up to date, ask to see the latest receipts or payments.

▶ Keys – find out how many sets of front door keys will be handed over. Ask to be given keys to all doors and gates, or instructions as to where they will be left at the property.

▶ Security alarm - if there is one, find out the security code.

▶ Confirm the date of vacancy - the property should be vacant from the

time of signing the deeds. The vendor has no right to remain in the property thereafter, but you may permit them to stay for a specified period of time whilst they arrange to leave. If so, it must be recorded in the private contract you sign.

▶ Last visit – arrange a time to visit the property with the vendor to find out how all the functional systems work.

▶ Local providers – ask for a comprehensive list of contact details from the vendor.

▶ Arrange insurance - you should be covered from the moment you sign the deeds.

Town houses on a new development. If you plan to buy a property, make sure you sort out your finances in advance.

Notary's fees
You may have to settle these before leaving if you have not made prior arrangements with your lawyer. If so, be sure to know what they will amount to and have the funds on you to pay them.

Signing the deeds before Notary

Notaries are required by law to run certain checks before they witness a deed of sale. For instance, they should request a *nota simple* to confirm that the vendor is the genuine owner of the property and it is is free of any (unexpected) encumbrances. This leads some agents to claim that buyers are well protected by the Notary and don't need a lawyer, but to protect your interests you *must* use your own lawyer, not only for the due diligence but also for accompanying you to the Notary. Your lawyer should already have passed to the Notary's clerk all the information required to prepare the deeds, and obtained a draft copy of them to check before signing; this avoids any potential delays. Signing the deeds is relatively straightforward, although it can feel a bit crowded and chaotic. Along with the Notary, all parties to the agreement must be present, which means everyone selling, everyone buying (or powers of attorney), any mortgage lenders, and lawyers from both sides. The estate agents or brokers involved are also likely to be present.

The procedure

Upon your arrival, you will be asked by the Notary's clerk for your identification before being shown into an office with all the parties involved to wait for the Notary. The Notary will start the proceedings by checking the vendors and buyers against their respective identity documents. Various details of your civil status may be confirmed along with your matrimonial status, if relevant.

The Notary will read the deeds aloud in Spanish, so you may not understand what is being said. This is not a problem if your lawyer is present. However, if you are not accompanied by a lawyer, you must take a translator along so that you know what you are signing. Some Notaries will refuse to sign the deeds if one or other of the parties does not understand Spanish and does not have a legal representative or translator present.

In the course of reading aloud the deeds, the Notary also confirms the payments made by the buyer to the vendor. This is when you produce payments, such as bank drafts for any outstanding amounts on the declared price (the price stated in the deeds less any deposits or down payments already paid). If you have agreed to pay a part of the price 'under the table' don't produce the cash in the presence of the Notary – wait until the deeds have been signed and the Notary has left the room.

If you are taking out a mortgage, this will require a separate deed, which the Notary will also read through. The latest IBI receipt and the certificate from the secretary of the community of owners will be checked to ensure that the vendor is up to date with these payments. Finally, the Notary informs the buyer and vendor of their fiscal obligations. If the vendor is a non-resident, the Notary will confirm that five per cent of the agreed price has been withheld by the buyer, to be paid to the Spanish tax authorities within 30 days.

If no objections have been raised by either party and if the payments are correct, then the deeds are passed round for signing by all parties and finally by the Notary. You are then handed the keys to your new property.

Once the deeds have been signed, the Notary will leave the room. If you are paying any money in cash, this is the time to hand it over to the vendor. Once this is done, the sale is complete and all that remains for you to do is to collect an unauthorized copy of the deeds (*copia simple*) from the Notary's clerk before leaving. There is a small charge for each copy and you should inform them of the number of copies you need in advance. The Notary will keep the original deeds (*copia autorizada*) for a few days in order to record them in their register, after which they can be collected by you for inscribing in the land register.

must know

What you need
You should take along your passport together with any cheques or cash, if you are paying this way, plus your NIE number. Although this is not essential for the signing, it will be needed within 30 days to pay the necessary taxes. It is also a good idea to have a few hundred euros in cash on you, as there may be petty expenses, such as sharing the IBI for the year, which can be paid direct to the vendor.

The sooner you inscribe your title in the land register the better; do it immediately after paying the ITP. You will need the original deeds (*copia autorizada*); a receipt to prove that ITP has been paid; a copy of the vendor's latest IBI receipt; a photocopy of your identity document; and an NIE number (or NIF number in some cases).

The inscription process should be completed within 15 days, after which the deeds can be collected. If the inscription fails for whatever reason you will be informed of this and told what you need to do to correct the problem and inscribe successfully. Once your title is inscribed in the property registry, the deeds can be collected. You may find it more convenient to have your lawyer keep them safe for you.

Updating the cadastre

You have to inform the cadastre that you are the new owner within two months of signing the deeds. Otherwise, the town hall will be unable to collect municipal rates (IBI), and if you fall behind with these payments your property can be embargoed and, ultimately, sold off. The property registry office and the Notary should inform the cadastre of your new title but they might not provide the information needed for collecting payments, so your lawyer or *gestor* should inform them as well. The most convenient place to update the cadastre is usually the town hall. Take along a *copia simple* plus a photocopy of your identity document and NIE number. You should provide your correspondence address (if different from the property) and your bank account details so that you can pay by standing order.

Utility contracts

After taking possession, sort out contracts with the utility companies: water, electricity, gas and telephone. Your cheapest and easiest option is to take over the vendor's contracts, thereby avoiding having to set up new contracts with each company. You need a recent copy of each utility bill from the vendor, so you can telephone each company. Quote the policy number on the bill, and change the name, correspondence address and bank account details to yours. You will also have to give each utility company your NIE number. It is usually possible to provide a correspondence address in the UK if that is where you wish to have the bills sent. Alternatively, visit the nearest consumer services office of each utility company or do it online.

Utility companies tend to charge on a bimonthly or quarterly basis, so it may be simpler to set up new contracts than try and coordinate the payments during the changeover period with the vendor (and risk being cut off). The procedure for this varies by utility company and region, but in most cases you can submit an application online or ring the company. Alternatively, you can visit their nearest consumer services office.

What you need

To set up new contracts, you will usually be asked to provide your name, NIE number or passport number, the address of the property, your bank account details and a *copia simple* of the deeds. When setting up contracts for a newly-built property you will also be asked to produce a first occupancy licence (*licencia de primera ocupación*). If you are asked to produce a document certifying that the property is habitable it will be the *cédula de habitabilidad*, which you can get from the town hall. It's a good idea to have several photocopies of your passport when dealing with utility companies as they may ask for this. Someone may have to read the meter, and you may be charged a fee for setting up each new contract.

want to know more?

Take it to the next level...

▶ **Buying off-plan** 146
▶ **Buying costs** 160
▶ **Financing your purchase** 172

Other sources...

▶ **For relevant articles, view *The Sunday Times* online at: www.timesonline.co.uk**
▶ **For resale properties direct from owners, see Vender Direct at: www.venderdirect.com**
▶ **For tools to help you manage your purchase and advice in the forum: www.spanishpropertyin sight.com**

8 Buying off-plan

Buying off-plan has been extremely popular in recent years, although many of the buyers have been off-plan investors rather than end users. By some estimates, up to 75 per cent of the purchases in popular areas like the Costa del Sol have been off-plan in recent years, although, of course, off-plan purchasing is limited to those areas where there are new developments. If you are considering buying an off-plan property, read the following chapter carefully so that you are aware of the pitfalls involved in buying a property this way.

Understanding the process

Buying off-plan requires a different approach from purchasing a resale property because you are buying from a developer, rather than a private individual, and because the property has not been built yet, which exposes you to an additional set of risks.

must know

Terms of use
If there are any communal facilities, such as a golf course, for which you have been promised special conditions of use, ensure that these conditions are attached as an addendum to the contract.

Negotiating with the developer

Many estate agents will try to persuade you to sign a reservation contract on the spot if you express any intention of buying an off-plan property. They often imply that the development is selling fast and you will miss the property, or the price will go up if you don't commit straight away. This might be true but they may be trying to deprive you of a 'cooling off' period during which you might have second

This example shows the type of artist's impression of a new property that will be provided to off-plan buyers by developers.

thoughts. Go away and think about it before you take the next step, and never sign a reservation contract without discussing it first with your lawyer.

After a cooling off period, if you decide you want to proceed, try to negotiate better terms with the developer rather than sign any contracts or make payments. Developers may be reluctant to give discounts but you won't get one if you don't ask. If you push, you might negotiate a discount off the list price, or more favourable payment terms, better fixtures or a furniture package. Trying to negotiate better terms from the developer once you have signed a reservation contract and paid a deposit is more difficult as it puts you in a weaker position.

It helps if the agent and developer think that you have seen alternatives and are basing your decision on the outcome of the negotiations. This is another reason for using several agents, as it can give you more leverage during negotiations. You don't have to be in Spain to carry out the negotiations or proceed to purchase. So long as you have a good lawyer in Spain you can do it all by phone, fax and email.

An example of a floor plan. You should always check plans very carefully.

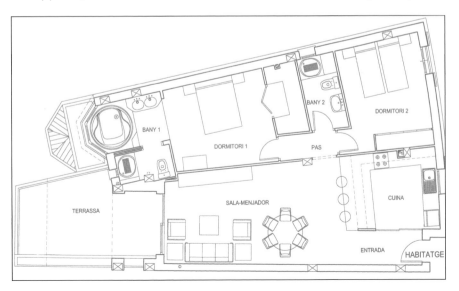

Reservation contract (*documento de reserva*)

When you have reached an agreement with the developer, you will be expected to sign a reservation contract and pay a deposit. Avoid doing this if possible. These contracts are usually vague and give little protection whilst requiring you to pay a lot of money for nothing more than the privilege of taking the property off the market for 30 days or so. It is less of a problem if the contract states that your deposit will be fully refunded if you decide not to proceed.

Due diligence

Regardless of whether you sign a reservation contract, the next step is a down payment contract, accompanied by the first payment (often 25 per cent of the price plus VAT). You may have to make further payments as the work progresses, with the final payment on signature of the deeds; or you may not have to make more payments until you sign the deeds when the property is completed. It depends on the terms agreed with the developer. Before committing to a down payment contract – often referred to as a private contract (*contrato privado de compraventa*) although the full name is *contrato de compraventa de vivienda en construcción* – get your lawyer to carry out a due diligence which is appropriate to buying off-plan.

Plans and specifications

Detailed plans (*planos*) and specifications (*memoria de calidades*) should be included in the contract you sign. The more detail there is, the more likely you are to get what you are expecting. Vague plans and specifications give developers a lot of flexibility that they might be tempted to use to deliver a smaller property or one of lower quality than you were expecting. After you have signed the contract and paid your money, the plans and specifications are all you have to prove what you have been promised. They should specify the built area (*superficie construida*), useable area (*superficie útil*) and total area, including common areas (*superficie total*). Note that in Spain, terraces are included in

> **must know**
>
> **Reserving a property**
> A reservation contract may be the only way to reserve a property in a buoyant market, but you are unlikely to lose out to another buyer if there is an over-supply. Some developers will agree to a clause enabling you to get your deposit back if you have a change of heart.

the figures at 50 per cent of their surface area. Also ask to see the technical plans that show the functional installations.

When buying an apartment, the plan of the building should clearly show the apartment you are purchasing. Otherwise you may find that it is in the middle of the second floor rather the corner of the third floor, as you had been led to believe. Unscrupulous agents and developers use this trick to make all the apartments appear to have the best position, in the hope that clients will then just put up with it when this turns out not to be the case.

Surroundings

People often focus on the property they are buying and forget about the developer's commitment to finish the surroundings. The landscaping will have an impact on the quality of life of the development. If corners are cut and developers do not fulfil their promises, some buyers may have to finish the job at their own expense. Plans for the surroundings should be well documented and attached as an addendum to the contract. Confirm that the communal facilities you have been promised, e.g. a swimming pool, are included in the plan authorized by the town hall (*cédula urbanística*), and are clearly stated in the overall deeds of the project (*escritura de la division horizontal*).

When buying off-plan you may be promised certain views. If there is land around the development that is not built on, check the *plan urbanístico* at the town hall to see what can and cannot be constructed on it. If an apartment block can be built in front of your property, assume that it will be.

Infrastructure

Find out what infrastructure the developer will put in place, and have your lawyer check the plans approved by the town hall to confirm this. If the developer fails to provide a plan that satisfies the town hall, the development may have problems receiving municipal services, which can make living there inconvenient and expensive.

Pay attention to the infrastructure for delivery of utilities, such as water, electricity, telephone and gas. Few developments outside of consolidated, built-up areas will have a mains gas connection, although most of Spain runs on bottled gas deliveries, which are likely to be cheaper if you are not buying a permanent home (you won't have to pay a monthly fixed charge when not using the property). The big problems are usually with water and electricity, which you can't live without. Before you buy, make sure there will be mains water and electricity connections, and do not take the developer's word for it. Your lawyer should check that the development has been fully approved by the town hall in this respect, and the developer has an approved construction licence (*licencia de construcción*). In this age of mobile phones and satellite broadband connections, one can live without a phone line but it is better to have one, so confirm a telephone connection will be available.

Community of owners

This normally gets going once the development has been sold and most of the buyers have completed. Always get your lawyer to look into the bylaws that the developer will establish for the community when first set up. Find out when it will be set up and how you can participate in its management.

Mortgage

Most developers have a prearranged mortgage that you can take over when you complete (see page 176). They save money if you do this and are likely to encourage you to do so. However, never accept the developer's mortgage without checking the conditions against other mortgages.

Land classification

Make sure the land on which the development is being built is classified for residential use, not 'tourist apartments', which can cause problems for buyers of holiday or permanent homes. Check the land classification with the town hall. Never buy on developments where the land is zoned for commercial or other types of use. Developers won't get building permission on this type of land although that has not stopped unscrupulous developers in areas like Marbella.

Planning permission

Check that the plans you are shown have been approved (*proyecto técnico aprobado*) and planning permission (*Licencia de construcción/edificación*) has been granted by the town hall. Never buy off-plan or on a new development

unless planning permission has already been granted. Many British buyers have made down payments of 30 per cent or more for property on developments that do not have and never will have planning permission. They were told that planning permission was just a formality that would be obtained without problems. Years later they are still waiting with their money tied up in a development that will never be built. This situation is more common on the Costa del Sol than on other coasts. To avoid this problem, ask your lawyer to confirm that planning permission has been granted for your specific building.

This aerial view shows a new golf development in Catalonia with an assortment of villas nestling around a golf course.

Regional urban plan

In the Marbella area, check that the development complies with the regional urban plan – request written confirmation from the town hall. Marbella's local administration has in the past granted illegal planning permission to a number of promoters, and some of these developments may be demolished now that the regional government in Seville is cracking down on corruption and illegal developments. Buyers who are innocent third parties are likely to receive little by way of compensation.

Developer's title to the land

Check the land registry to confirm that the land belongs to the developer, the building project has been inscribed, and what debts or charges are secured against the property. Most developers use mortgage financing so a debt against the land is not necessarily a problem.

Stage payment guarantees

The law obliges developers taking stage payments for off-plan properties to take out insurance (*póliza de seguro*) or a bank guarantee (*aval bancario*) to protect these funds and any interest they earn whilst in their possession. However, some don't bother with it or take out insufficient cover. Before handing over any money, ask for proof that this has been arranged. When you sign the down payment contract, get a document from the guarantor specifying that your payments are guaranteed (using your name). If you have any doubts, ask your lawyer and contact the bank or insurance company providing the guarantee. Some developers claim they are 'in the process of arranging the insurance'. You should not make any stage payments until they can prove that the insurance has been arranged.

must know

Special accounts
Developers in Spain are required by law to isolate your stage payments in a special account which is used only for paying for building work related to your property. Before making any payments, you should confirm that the developer has a special client account and, if possible, you should also have a clause included in the contract that commits them to comply with this law.

Reviewing the down payment contract

Before you sign the contract (or make any payments) your lawyer should check that it balances your interests with those of the developer. Many standard contracts drawn up by developers are weighted heavily in their favour. Any contract that you sign should include the following:

▶ Detailed description identifying the developer.
▶ Detailed description identifying the buyer.
▶ Description of the project and the land, stating the developer's title to the land and any debts inscribed with it.
▶ The constructor and technical architect should be identified.

▶ Detailed description of the property, including plans and specifications.
▶ The price agreed, specifying the VAT.
▶ A detailed stage payment calendar giving specific dates or milestones, and details of the bank account to which payments should be made, plus details of how building milestones will be certified, i.e. architect's signature.
▶ A specific date by which the property will be finished, an extension period (if any), and the financial penalty the developer has to pay for every day of delay beyond this period. The contract should also state that the buyer can withdraw from the contract, receiving a full refund plus interest, if the developer fails to meet the deadlines specified.
▶ The percentage of the payments you will lose if you fail to complete. Try and limit this to 40 per cent or less.
▶ A clause stating that the developer will meet all transaction costs that relate to them (e.g. the Notary costs of declaring a newly-built property known as the *escritura de obra nueva y division horizontal*, and the *plusvalía*).
▶ Details of the insurance or bank guarantee to protect the stage payments, naming the policy number and financial institution providing the guarantee.
▶ What information will be provided in the specifications manual (*libro del edificio*) which must be given to the buyer on completion.
▶ A clause listing the addendum to the contract.
▶ How the costs related to setting up the utilities will be apportioned.
▶ The correspondence address and contact details of both parties, for all communication during the life of the contract.

Waiting for completion

Once your lawyer has carried out an appropriate due diligence and helped you negotiate a strong contract you can proceed to sign and make the first payment, often between 10 and 25 per cent (plus VAT) of the price.

Signing the private sale contract

This is the point of no return beyond which you cannot back out of buying the property without incurring some heavy financial penalties, probably involving the loss of some or all of your stage payments, depending upon what has been agreed in the contract.

You do not need to be physically present in Spain in order to sign this contract. A contract signed by the developer can be faxed to you for countersigning and returned by fax. However, signed originals also need to be exchanged by post. Both you and the developer should end up with original copies which have been signed by both parties.

Stage payments and construction

Once you have signed the private sale contract and made the first payment there is not much for you to do until completion approaches. During this period, which could last up to two years, construction of your property will be underway and you may be required to make a series of stage payments as agreed with the developer in the contract.

If you are required to make further payments, do make sure that you receive an official receipt from the developer detailing these. Many developers tend to be very bad at keeping buyers informed of construction progress. It is in your interests to push the developer to send you regular progress reports and also to provide plenty of warning if there are any changes to the expected date of delivery.

Final legal checks

When the property is completed you can take possession by signing the public deeds before a Notary. Before doing this your lawyer will need to carry out a series of final checks, including the following:

▶ Confirm that the property has been certified as finished by a registered architect (*certificado de final de obras*).

▶ Confirm that the property has been, or will be given, a first occupancy licence by the local government (*licencia de primera ocupación*). An official from the planning department of the municipal authority will inspect the finished property to ensure it complies with regulations. If it conforms, it will be granted the appropriate licence. Without this, you cannot get a mortgage or have utilities connected.

▶ Request a land registry filing for your specific property to check there are no unexpected debts or embargoes on it. The promoter should have signed deeds before a Notary (*escritura de obra nueva y division horizontal*) that register the division of the original land into the individual properties and common areas. So the property you are buying should be inscribed in the land registry and you can check its status. Do not sign any deeds before your lawyer has checked the land registry filing (*nota simple*).

▶ Confirm with the town hall that the property has no outstanding debts, such as unpaid taxes, or any other issues that might cause problems.

▶ Check that the necessary insurance has been arranged by the developer to cover build defects, as required by the building regulations law (*ley de ordenación de la edificación*). Developers are obliged to insure any minor defects for one year, more substantial defects related to fixtures and fittings for three years, and structural defects for 10 years. This insurance should form part of the property manual (*libro del edificio*) that the developer gives you.

Making a will

It is a good idea to have a will drawn up in Spain if you are going to own a property there. This can be done by your lawyer. You may have to consult a specialist tax adviser to explain the inheritance tax implications.

Property broker fee

If you buy through an estate agent the fee is usually paid by the vendor, but you should always clarify this in advance to avoid any unpleasant surprises. If you use a buyer's agent you will be expected to pay a fee for their service, often of two-and-a-half per cent of the transaction price of the property.

Furniture

Never forget that you will need to furnish the property. If you have furniture in the UK that you can use in your new Spanish home, remember that you will incur shipping costs transporting it to Spain. Many companies in Spain offer furniture packages in newly-built homes, which for a typical two-bed apartment start at around 12,000 to 15,000 euros.

Main conveyancing costs in euros

Property value or mortgage loan value	Property taxes		Property expenses		Mortgage expenses		
	Resale build	New build	Notary	Registry	Notary	Registry	Stamp duty
50,000	3,500	4,000	350	150	430	150	690
100,000	7,000	8,000	440	200	490	230	1.500
200,000	14,000	16,000	540	350	630	330	3.300
300,000	21,000	24,000	600	390	670	380	4.800
400,000	28,000	32,000	720	430	730	430	6,500
500,000	35,000	40,000	800	470	780	480	8,400
600,000	42,000	48,000	900	520	840	540	9,900
1,000,000	70,000	80,000	1,000	721	1,000	740	17,650

All the figures above are rough estimates only.

Utility set-up costs

If you buy a new property you will have to set up new utility contracts. A very approximate guide to the costs of doing this yourself are as follows:

▶ Gas: 70 euros
▶ Telephone: 130 euros
▶ Water: 120 euros
▶ Electricity: 100 euros

Main conveyancing costs

The table (right) gives an approximate idea of the main fixed conveyancing costs, but does not include the other important costs, such as legal fees, banking costs and foreign exchange expenses, which will depend upon the terms that you agree with the respective providers.

As you can see from this table, if you were to buy a 300,000 euro property in Andalusia with a mortgage of 200,000 euros, then your fixed conveyancing costs would be something in the region of nine to ten per cent, depending upon whether you were buying a new-build or a resale property.

You should bear in mind, however, that these figures are just indicative, and they are only provided to help you draw up a budget and understand the costs that you can expect to pay during the purchase process. The actual costs can vary considerably from case to case.

Conveyancing cost examples

Resale property, Andalusia

Property value	300,000
Mortgage value	200,000

EXPENSE	COST €
Tax	21,000
Notary fee property deed	600
Registry fee property deed	390
Notary fee mortgage deed	630
Registry fee mortgage deed	330
Stamp duty on mortgage	3,300
TOTAL EXPENSES	26,250
Total as % of property price	9%

New-build property, Andalusia

Property value	300,000
Mortgage value	200,000

EXPENSE	COST €
Tax	24,000
Notary fee property deed	600
Registry fee property deed	390
Notary fee mortgage deed	630
Registry fee mortgage deed	330
Stamp duty on mortgage	3,300
TOTAL EXPENSES	29,250
Total as % of property price	10%

The cost of ownership

Property is a demanding asset in terms of both ownership and maintenance costs. The bigger and more expensive the property you own, the higher the taxes and running costs you will face.

Taxes

When you own property in Spain you have to pay the local rates (IBI), a wealth tax (*Patrimonio*) and income tax (IRPF if resident, and IRNR if non-resident). The wealth tax and income tax will vary according to your residency status and whether or not you rent out your property. Your lawyer or a fiscal advisor will help you find out or estimate these taxes before you buy a property.

You are strongly advised to appoint a fiscal representative in Spain to handle all your tax payments. If you fail to pay your taxes you will be fined, and in the worst case scenario your property can

Municipal property tax - Municipal rates (IBI)	
Spanish name	*Impuesto sobre Bienes Inmuebles* (IBI)
Description	This tax is the Spanish equivalent of the rates and is collected by local government. All property owners in Spain pay this tax.
Tax base and rate	The tax base is the cadastral value of the property and the rate varies from 0.4 to 1.1 per cent for residential property (*urbana*), depending upon the region. The tax rate can be as low as 0.3 per cent for agricultural property, or higher than 1.1 per cent under certain circumstances. You can find out the tax rate for a specific property from the vendor or the town hall.
Form	N/A
Dates	Payment period determined by the local authority. In many cases this tax is collected in September.
Example	Varies, but 200–500 euros per annum is common.

even be seized and sold off by the authorities to pay the taxes due. If a non-resident owns more than one property in Spain they are obliged by law to appoint a fiscal representative. If you have only one property but have more than one set of deeds (if the garage has a different set of deeds, for example), you are considered to own two properties and have to appoint a fiscal representative.

Wealth tax	
Spanish name	*Impuesto sobre el Patrimonio (Patrimonio)*
Description	Everyone who owns property in Spain (residents and non-residents alike) has to pay an annual wealth tax based on the net value of their assets in Spain after permitted deductions, such as mortgages. This tax is collected by regional governments. Residents are allowed certain deductions, but non-residents are not.
Tax base and rate	The tax is based on the net value of your property (less mortgage, if any) or another value deemed appropriate by the tax authorities. The tax rate works on a sliding scale of tax bands with marginal rates starting at 0.2 per cent and rising to 2.5 per cent for assets worth over 10.7 million Euros. The first 108,200 euros is exempt of tax for residents; 150,253 euros is exempt for a principal residency. There is no exemption for non-residents, who will pay tax on the full net value of their assets.
Form	714
Dates	Presented during June for previous calendar year.
Example	A non-resident with a property valued at 300,000 euros and no mortgage in Spain would pay approx. 700 euros per annum. A non-resident with a property valued at 300,000 euros and a 70 per cent mortgage in Spain would pay approximately 180 euros per annum. A resident with a principal home valued at 300,000 euros and no mortgage in Spain would pay approximately 300 euros per annum. A resident with a principal home valued at 300,000 euros and a 70 per cent mortgage in Spain would not have to pay any wealth tax.

Income tax for non-residents

Non-residents who do not rent out their property (standard declaration)

Spanish name	*Impuesto sobre la renta de no residentes, declaración ordinaria* (IRNR)
Description	You pay this version of income tax in Spain if the following conditions apply: 1) you do not reside in Spain; 2) you own property in Spain; 3) the property is exclusively for personal use and you do not rent it out; or 4) you have no other source of taxable income in Spain. Although you do not earn an income from the property, in the eyes of the Spanish tax authorities you still derive a benefit from owning a property in Spain and therefore have to pay an imputed income tax.
Tax base and rate	Tax base: 1.1% of the cadastral value (or 2 per cent if the cadastral value has not been subject to revision or modification sine 1st January 1994). Tax rate: 25 per cent.
Form	210
Dates	Presented before the 30th June each year. For example, you have from 1st January to 30th June 2006 to declare tax on income during 2005.
Example	Cadastral value of property = 200,000 euros; base = 2,200 euros Tax = 25% x 2,200 euros = 550 euros

Income tax for non-residents

Non-residents who do not rent out their properties combined with the wealth tax

Spanish name	*Impuesto sobre la renta de no residentes, y Patrimonio (IRNR y Patrimonio)*
Description	Under certain conditions, non-residents can pay the two taxes mentioned above (IRNR and *Patrimonio*) in the same declaration and using the same form. This is not an extra tax, just a more convenient way of paying the two taxes. To present them together in the same form you have to meet the following conditions: 1) you do not reside in Spain; 2) you only own one property in Spain; and 3) this property is exclusively for personal use and not rented out.
Tax base and rate	The value of the tax is the sum of the two taxes as explained above.
Form	214
Dates	Presented any time during the following calendar year. So you present in 2006 for taxes in 2005.
Example	N/A

Income tax for non-residents

Non-residents who rent out their property

Spanish name	*Impuesto sobre la renta de no residentes, declaración ordinaria* (IRNR)
Description	If you: 1) do not reside in Spain; 2) own property in Spain; and 3) rent out your property, you have to pay income tax on the rent instead of the imputed tax. If you rent out your property to a Spanish company, the company will deduct tax at source and pay it to the tax authorities. In this case a non-resident is not obliged to present the forms 210 or 215. However, if you rent your property to anyone other than a Spanish company you have to declare and pay income tax.
Tax base and rate	The tax base is the gross rent, with no deductions allowed, and the tax rate is 25 per cent.
Form	210 or 215
Dates	210 = monthly, one month after rent is due; 215 = quarterly, in the first 20 days of the month following the end of the quarter.
Example	Annual gross rental income of 20,000 euros Tax @ 25% = 5,000 euros

Income tax for residents

Spanish name	*Impuesto sobre la renta de las personas físicas* (IRPF)
Description	Ordinary income tax that all Spanish residents have to pay. This is not a property tax and depends entirely upon your income and fiscal circumstances.

Other ownership costs

Taxes are not the only expense that you will have to meet as a consequence of owning a property in Spain. You will almost certainly have to pay some utility, maintenance and cleaning costs, depending on the type of property that you buy, its size, characteristics, location and use. Overleaf are the typical additional costs that you may face; before buying a property, make sure you quantify these costs so that you know what kind of an ongoing financial commitment you are taking on.

Community fees

If the property you buy is part of a community of owners then you will have to pay your share of the annual community fees (*cuota*). You can find out what the annual *cuota* is for any property that you are considering buying or have bought from the secretary or administrator of the community.

Insurance

You are strongly advised to take out building insurance; if you use a mortgage your lender will insist that you do so. Insurance premiums in Spain are considerably lower than in the UK, and you can get a quote rapidly from a broker. Find out what

information insurance companies require to prepare a quote, and gather this during one of your visits, or from the estate agent. Consider taking out contents insurance, and mortgage insurance if applicable. If you plan to rent out your property your insurance policy should reflect this.

Utilities

The owner of a rural property with a private well, solar panels, butane tank deliveries, a mobile phone and broadband satellite internet connection will not have to pay any utility charges. However, most British people who own properties in villages or urbanizations will have to pay for water, electricity, gas and a telephone line. All utility connections involve a fixed fee for the connection, and a variable charge according to use. When buying a resale property, find out the utility running costs from the vendor.

Maintenance

All properties incur cleaning and maintenance costs, and these will depend upon their size, age and location. A garden and a pool will also increase the time and expense of looking after a property. In many areas where the British tend to buy, there are specialist companies that offer a full cleaning and maintenance service.

Rental management

If you rent out your property you will need to hire a company to manage its marketing and rental, although it is now possible to do some of the marketing and booking yourself via the websites that have sprung up to offer this service. If you use a local company to provide you with the full service, you will probably have to pay them around 30 per cent or more of the gross rental income. As a non-resident, you will not be able to deduct any of this fee for tax purposes.

Mortgage payments

If you take out a mortgage to buy your property, then you will have to pay monthly mortgage payments. These will depend upon the conditions of the mortgage that you have taken out.

Arranging your finances

Sound financial arrangements will need to be made if you are to enjoy a successful purchase, and it is surprising how few people seem to address the financial side of things in a structured and organized way. Here is some advice on how to go about it.

Issues to address

The better you understand and arrange your finances, the more financially comfortable you are likely to be with the purchase over the long term. Furthermore, by carefully evaluating your finances and optimizing the way in which you structure the purchase, you may be able to spend more on a property than you thought, and still not place your finances under unreasonable stress. There are three financial issues to address before you buy:

▶ Work out an accurate property budget, taking into account your own funds, how much you can sensibly borrow, and the costs of the purchase.

▶ Estimate and plan for the ongoing financial commitments that you take on when you buy a property in Spain. These may be in addition to your living costs in the UK, or instead of these costs if you are relocating permanently to Spain. Whatever your situation, you don't want these costs to take you by surprise.

▶ Unless your finances (savings and earnings) are in euros, you need to understand and manage your exchange rate exposure, both for the purchase and for ongoing commitments.

Work out your property budget
Your objective is to work out the maximum you can afford to spend on a property without putting your finances under stress. If you use a mortgage you will not know your exact budget until you have had the property you want to buy valued, which can sometimes cause problems. Therefore you should always be

conservative in your assumptions. The table (right) will help you to organize your budget. Firstly, you need to calculate the funds you have at your disposal, then search for a property that matches your budget, bearing in mind the transaction costs involved. Once you have found a property, you need to be sure that your numbers still add up, given any extra costs. It is important to establish a clear budget at the outset and keep funds in reserve for unforeseen expenses. However, your budget may change as your search proceeds. You may, for instance, be able to borrow more or less than expected based on the property valuation that is carried out by the bank, or refurbishment costs may be higher than you expected. Whatever happens, you have to keep a firm grip on the numbers to avoid serious problems.

Working out your ownership budget

You should also estimate the ongoing financial commitment you are taking on. The bigger and more expensive the property, the higher the ownership costs will be. The table overleaf on page 174 serves to identify the costs you will need to estimate and plan for.

If you are planning to rent out your property for part of the year to help meet your ownership costs, you must estimate your rental income and related expenses.

Your purchase budget
FUNDING
Own funds
Mortgage borrowing
Total funds
PROPERTY EXPENSES
Property price
Legal
Tax
Notary and register
Total property expenses
MORTGAGE EXPENSES
Mortgage opening
Valuation
Administrative fee
Stamp duty
Total mortgage expenses
TOTAL EXPENSES
OTHER EXPENSES TO CONSIDER
Banking charges: for receiving international transfers and issuing bank guaranteed cheques.
Survey: fees for a standard survey are often around 0.1% of the property's value, with a minimum of 400 euros for a valuation, rising to 600 euros for a building survey.
Moving costs: these vary. If they are likely to be substantial, try to quantify them before committing to a purchase.
Furniture
Utilities
Refurbishment
Buyer's agent fee: approx. 2.5%, if applicable

Ownership budget

ITEM	COMMENTS
Taxes	Income tax and wealth tax
Local rates	IBI. Often between 300 and 800 euros per annum (p.a.)
Community fees	Often between 300 and 1,000 euros p.a. depending upon the development. Not applicable if no community of owners.
Gestoria	Cost of outsourcing tax declarations and payments. Often around 300 euros p.a.
Utilities	Depends upon property and use.
Maintenance and cleaning	Depends upon property and use.
Insurance	Depends upon policy cover. Often between 300 and 500 euros p.a.
Mortgage payments	Depends upon mortgage value and terms.

RENTAL ISSUES

Rental income	Work on the basis of conservative assumptions.
Rental expenses	Marketing costs, rental management costs, utilities and depreciation.
Tax on gross income	25% for non-residents, no deductions allowed.
Net rental income	Gross income less rental expenses less tax.

Estate agents often overstate rental potential and understate the related costs, so do your research if rental potential is critical to your budget. At the very least, talk to independent rental agents in the area.

Managing exchange rate exposure
Unless your savings or income are in euros, you must take care as exchange rate fluctuations can either increase or decrease your financial commitments substantially in a short period of time. In a recent five-year period, the pound/euro exchange rate has swung by up to 30 per cent, which at its most extreme could have made a 300,000 euro property 47,000 pounds more expensive for a British buyer.

Exchange rate exposures can be particularly problematic when you make stage payments over many months. In the table opposite we take the stage payments involved in an off-plan purchase for a 300,000 euro property and show the impact of euro/sterling exchange rate movements over time on the overall price. Because the pound weakened against the euro during this period, the property ended up eight per cent (£13,854) more expensive than it had been when the buyer signed the purchase contract and took on the euro liability.

Exchange rate risks for stage payments

Exchange		Date	euros	rate	pounds
Exposure at beginning of contract		1-Jan-02	300,000	1.6337	183,632
1st payment	20%	1-Jan-02	60,000	1.6337	36,726
2nd payment	20%	1-Jun-02	60,000	1.5605	38,449
3rd payment	20%	1-Sep-02	60,000	1.5795	37,987
4th payment	20%	1-Mar-03	60,000	1.4579	41,155
Final payment	20%	1-Jun-03	60,000	1.3899	43,169
Total paid by completion			300,000		197,486
Difference due to exchange rate					13,854

This example has been chosen due to the high fluctuation in exchange rates in this period.

Of course, it works both ways and if the pound had strengthened against the euro during this period the buyer would have ended up paying less in sterling. However, most buyers have to work within their budgets and need to be certain at the time of signing the purchase contract how much the property is going to cost them in pounds. This is as true for buyers signing a private contract with completion in two months' time as it is for an off-plan buyer with completion in two years' time.

Most people cannot afford to have exchange rates go against them, which means fixing the exchange rate when taking on a euro liability (or buying euros on the spot). The best way to reduce exchange rate uncertainty is to use financial instruments, such as forward contracts, that help you to manage your exchange rate risk.

A good currency broker will be able to explain recent trends and advise you on the best exchange rate strategy given your circumstances. Don't buy your euros through a high street bank as they tend to offer uncompetitive rates that can add thousands of pounds onto the cost of your purchase.

Once you own your property, you will probably need to transfer funds to Spain on a regular basis to meet your ownership costs. Discuss this with a currency broker and make the necessary arrangements to ensure regular transfers at the best rates.

Mortgages

You will need a mortgage unless you are a cash buyer. Even if you have enough cash it may be in your interests to use a mortgage, so evaluate this before searching for a property. A mortgage can provide potential fiscal benefits, increased security of purchase resulting from the lender's due diligence, and higher returns on your investment (due to leverage) if your property's value increases. The downsides are the cost of taking one out, and the need to have cash available to meet payments now and in the future (when interest rates might be higher).

Decide at the outset whether you want a mortgage, and whether you wish to take one out in Spain or the UK. If you want one, start making the arrangements almost before you do anything else. There are also some advantages in doing so:

▶ You have time to examine the question in depth and consider your options, which helps you take better decisions and avoid overpaying.

▶ You go into your property search with a clearer idea of your budget.

▶ You have a better chance of finding a mortgage with the best conditions; otherwise you may end up with an expensive and inflexible mortgage.

▶ You reduce the risk of losing a property which has cost so much to find.

Raising the finance

As the overseas property market has developed so too have the financing options. You should contact mortgage brokers in both the UK and Spain, and ask them to explain the advantages and disadvantages of taking out different mortgages and the conditions they offer, before deciding which option best fits your circumstances. The advantages and disadvantages of each option are set out in the table opposite.

Each alternative has to be evaluated in the light of your particular circumstances, but remortgaging a UK property usually works out cheaper for short-term mortgages of, say, between five and 10 years, whilst a new mortgage in Spain may work out cheaper over longer periods (depending on euro/sterling interest rate differentials). However, if you do decide to take out a mortgage in Spain you have to

Mortgage advantages and disadvantages

Type of mortgage	Advantages	Disadvantages
Euro mortgage on Spanish property from Spanish bank	▶ Asset and liability in same currency. ▶ Better match between rental income and mortgage payments. ▶ Some fiscal advantages.	▶ Expensive set-up and switching costs. ▶ Repayments have to be made in euros in Spain. ▶ Potential complications of dealing with Spanish bank.
Euro mortgage on Spanish property from UK bank	▶ Asset and liability in same currency.	▶ Expensive set-up and switching costs. ▶ Repayments subject to exchange rate exposure. ▶ Potentially high administrative costs. ▶ Risk of uncompetitive exchange rates.
Sterling mortgage on Spanish property from UK bank	▶ Repayments in sterling an option. ▶ Dealing with UK bank. ▶ Some fiscal advantages.	▶ Expensive set-up and switching costs. ▶ Repayments subject to exchange rate exposure. ▶ Asset and liability in different currencies.
Remortgage UK property in sterling from UK bank	▶ Cheap set-up and switching costs. ▶ Repayments in sterling; no exchange rate exposure on monthly payments. ▶ Dealing with UK bank.	▶ Requires having a suitable property in the UK. ▶ Asset and liability in different currencies.

make sure that you select a mortgage with favourable conditions, as the high set-up and switching costs of Spanish mortgages mean that mistakes are much more expensive to undo than in the UK. It is very important that you deal with a trustworthy and experienced mortgage broker who will not try to sell you an expensive and inflexible mortgage for a higher commission.

Taking out a mortgage in Spain

The Spanish mortgage market is fiercely competitive with many lenders to choose from. Some do have staff who can deal with English-speaking clients, but generally they are not well placed to manage applications from British buyers. Most big British banks also lend mortgages in Spain, along with offering sterling mortgages on Spanish properties.

Mortgage brokers

Given the complexity of the product, the difference in terms and conditions on offer, and your need to deal with fluent English speakers who will understand your circumstances, you are usually better off dealing with a mortgage broker who specializes in helping British buyers. They charge a fee, usually between a half and two per cent of the loan, and some also charge an administrative fee to evaluate your application. If you work with a mortgage broker the application process is quite straightforward.

▶ You fill in an appraisal form to enable your broker to evaluate your financial circumstances and provide an estimate of how much you can borrow.

▶ Assuming your case is viable, you will be asked to provide documents, such as pay slips and tax returns, to confirm your financial circumstances. If you have not yet found a property, leave the mortgage process on standby at this stage until you are ready. If you have already found a property, you will also be asked to provide details about it, such as a *nota simple*.

▶ Your broker will submit your application to the lenders most likely to offer you the best conditions given your requirements, and will arrange for a valuation of the property to be carried out by a company approved by all the lenders, on the strength of which each lender will make you an official written offer. Discuss the pros and cons of each offer with your broker.

▶ In most cases, official offers are valid for one month, but sometimes for three months. You must coordinate the signing of the deeds with your broker and the vendor to ensure this takes place whilst the offer is still valid.

▶ Before signing the deeds your broker will help you set up an account with the selected mortgage lender and you will need to transfer the funds to meet the costs of the transaction not covered by the mortgage. This will include your equity capital, taxes, fees and mortgage set-up costs.

▶ After the deeds have been signed your mortgage lender will take charge of paying the taxes (funds provided by you) and inscribing the title and mortgage in the land register. You will then start making your monthly mortgage payments.

Mortgage facts in Spain

▶ Banks will lend up to 70 per cent for second homes, depending on your age and financial circumstances. They may even be prepared to lend up to 100 per cent to fiscal residents buying a principal home.

▶ Spanish residents can get 35-year mortgages (depending upon age), with the possibility of 40-year mortgages imminent. Non-residents are normally only offered a maximum of 30 years.

▶ Banks only allow you to take out mortgage commitments of a maximum of 35 per cent of your net (after tax) income. If you already have a mortgage in the UK or elsewhere, then your existing repayments will be included in this figure. Some banks will allow you to go to 40 per cent of net income.

▶ Opening (arrangement) fees in Spain are often between one and one-and-a-half per cent.

▶ Variable mortgage rates are often Euribor plus one per cent. Euribor is the euro-zone interest rate used to calculate mortgage rates in Spain.

▶ Fixed-rate and interest-only mortgages are uncommon in Spain but they can be found.

▶ Cancellation fees are often one per cent for total early redemption. Partial redemption fees are negotiable.

▶ The fee for changing mortgage lenders is often half a per cent.

▶ If you take out a mortgage in Spain you pay an administrative fee (*gestor*) for paying taxes and inscribing the mortgage and title in the property register.

▶ You will not get a mortgage for more than the value declared in the deeds, so bear this in mind if you agree to pay any amount under the table.

▶ Banks usually have much stricter lending limits for rural properties, and are unlikely to lend more than 40 to 50 per cent of the price in such cases.

▶ Beware of mortgage brokers promising 100 per cent mortgages. Some of them charge up to 1,000 euros or more to study or process your application but have no intention of getting you a mortgage. This is basically a scam.

Investing in Spanish property

Most people are looking for a home or holiday property that will also serve as a good investment, and many plan to rent it out when not using it. However, some have started speculating with off-plan purchases, leading an increasing number into financial distress.

Capital appreciation outlook

The new breed of off-plan speculators apart, most of the British people buying property in Spain are not expecting to make a fortune from their property. In most cases they merely hope that the real value of their property will rise with time, and that at the very least they won't end up out of pocket in real terms (taking into account inflation and transaction costs) when they sell. After all, the main 'return on investment' will come from the value of the property as a home – a place to enjoy living in – and although this return is difficult to quantify, it will be real and substantial.

But even if making money is not the main priority for most British buyers, most still pray for substantial capital gains over time. The purchase may be part of a pension plan, or looking further ahead they may need to sell their Spanish property one day to help finance a return to the United Kingdom for their final years, or to provide for the inheritance of their family. So what are the perspectives for Spanish property price increases in the future?

The first thing to make clear is that nobody knows for sure what will happen to Spanish property prices in future. All we can be sure of is that Spanish property has been a good investment in the recent past, with 12 consecutive years of price increases, and prices up 89 per cent over four years to the end of 2004. However, this trend cannot go on forever and, realistically, the

Spanish economy's capacity to absorb large property price increases has probably been used up for the time being. But whilst Spanish property is unlikely to continue to be a 'growth stock', it is reasonable to expect that real values will continue to increase over the long term (or at least not fall), whilst providing owners with other types of value, such as a home they can live in and enjoy.

Off-plan speculation

In the short term, however, some of the most popular coastal areas, such as the Costa del Sol, appear to be entering a downturn, in which speculative investors are losing money and prices are stagnating or declining. Bad timing is causing problems for many of the British off-plan speculators who have recently bought in the hope of earning high tax-free profits (as promised by estate agents) by selling on before completion. This misguided speculation by credulous amateur investors partly explains why there are now too many properties chasing too few buyers, and why investors are finding it difficult or impossible to sell on before completion.

Investors are also finding that the estate agents who were so eager to sell them the investments in the first place are not interested in helping them sell on and realize their investments (the commissions are not high enough). Rash investors who have over-extended and cannot afford to complete have to sell on at any price – usually a loss – or lose all of their payments to date. This further depresses prices. The next few years may be a good time to pick up a coastal property at a discount, but do not be tempted to speculate with off-plan property.

Renting out property

Many of the people buying holiday or semi-permanent homes in Spain also plan to rent out their property when not using it. Doing so can generate an income to contribute towards the property maintenance and financing costs, and in some cases may even enable people to buy a more expensive property than they might otherwise have been able to afford. However, there are some important things to understand before anyone proceeds to buy a property on the assumption of easy and substantial rental income.

Firstly, estate agents tend to exaggerate the rental potential of the properties they are trying to sell, which is a standard way to convince people to buy a property that they cannot afford. It is quite common for buyers to be assured of 25 to 30 weeks' rental a year, when five to ten weeks is more realistic. So if rental potential is important to you, then always check the rental expectations and rates for a property you are considering with an independent rental agent before proceeding to buy. Note that at the present time there is an over-supply of both rental apartments and hotel beds on many of Spain's most popular coasts, which is driving down occupancy rates, rental income and yields for all but the best rental properties.

Another unexpected problem that many buyers encounter is the surprisingly high cost of renting out property in Spain, especially for non-residents. If you do everything by the book and rent out the property legally and officially, then as a non-resident you have to pay 25 per cent of the gross rent in tax, with no deductible expenses allowed, and in some areas may also have to pay for a local government licence to rent out property on a short-term or 'tourist' basis.

Then there is the marketing agency fee (for providing clients) and the property management fee (for looking after the property, cleaning before and after guests, etc.), which combined often amount to 40 per cent or more of the gross rental income. So if you rent out your property legally – you declare your rental income – then at least half of the gross rental income is likely to go on income tax, marketing fees and management fees. In many cases that does not leave you with much to contribute to other costs, such as a mortgage, and may not compensate you for the extra hassles involved in renting out your property. That is why so many people limit their rentals to family and friends (cash only) with no tax declaration.

There is always the option of saving costs by trying to market and manage the property yourself, using the internet sites that have emerged in the last few years to make this option more viable. However, most people don't have time to do this, let alone the knowledge of the relevant operational or legal aspects, and many who have attempted to do so express serious reservations about its payback. Renting your property to strangers can involve aggravation and damage to your property, as well as clients who fail to pay, and so on. And as everyone in the rental business knows, short-term holiday tenants are the most difficult clients. So think hard before attempting to manage your own rentals, but if you rent through a company always use a serious, established company as there are many cowboys in the rental business, and dealing with unprofessional companies is risky.

Buy-to-let

Buying-to-let means investing in property with the sole intention of renting it out. This has been a very popular investment strategy in the UK but is much less popular in Spain, where the law, in protecting tenants at the expense of landlords, does not encourage owners to rent out their property. This explains why there are three million empty properties and an under-developed rental market in Spain.

Unless you are experienced in renting out property in Spain you would be well advised to avoid investing in buy-to-let properties there. Spanish law makes it more risky to be a landlord there than in the UK, and, furthermore, rental yields have reached dismal lows for the time being. There are some guaranteed-rental schemes to be found when you are buying on new developments (also known as leasebacks, though genuine leasebacks on the French model do not exist in Spain), which can offer investors a neater solution for investing in both property and a rental income. However, you should always study carefully the small print on these schemes, as their terms can be quite unattractive once you go beyond the headline advantages outlined in the brochure.

want to know more?

Take it to the next level...

▶ **Getting ready to buy** 64
▶ **Buying previously-owned property** 110
▶ **Buying off-plan** 146

Other sources...
▶ **The Spanish Mortgage Association** publishes data on mortgage rates in Spain. View at: **www.ahe.es**
▶ **Spanish Government tax authority** provides guides in English to taxes in Spain: **www.aeat.es**
▶ **Financial evaluations, models and examples** are to be found on: **www.spanishpropertyinsight.com**

Glossary

SPANISH	ENGLISH
Abogado	Lawyer, solicitor
Administrador de la comunidad de propietarios	Administrator of the community of owners
Apartamento	Apartment
API – *Agentes de la Propiedad Inmobiliaria*	Estate agent belonging to the official organization of estate agents
Aval bancario	Bank guarantee
Casa adosada	Semi-detached property or terraced town house
Casa de pueblo	Village house
Casa rural	Rural property
Catastro	The cadastre, a record of all properties for tax and administrative purposes
Cédula de habitabilidad or *licencia de primera ocupación*	Occupancy licence from the town hall
Cédula urbanística	Urban planning report from the town hall
Certificación sobre las deudas con la Comunidad de Propietarios	Certificate that community of owners payments are up to date
Certificado de antigüedad	Certificate issued by an architect confirming the age of a building
Certificado de final de obras	Certificate issued by an architect confirming that a property has been completed according to the approved plans
Certificado literal de dominio y cargas	Detailed property registry filing
Chalet	Detached property
Cheque bancaria	Bank guaranteed cheque
Colegio de abogados	Professional association of lawyers
Comunidad de propietarios	Community of owners
Contrato de compraventa de vivienda en construcción	Private purchase contract of a property under construction
Contrato de opción de compra	Option to buy contract

SPANISH	ENGLISH
Contrato privado de arras penitenciales	Deposit contract
Contrato privado de compraventa	Private purchase contract
Contrato privado de paga y señal	Down payment contract
Copia autorizada	Authorized copy of the deeds signed by the Notary
Copia simple	Copy of the deeds
Corredore	Broker, rural property broker
Cortijo	Country property (south of Spain)
Cuota	Community fees
Derecho inmobiliario	Real estate law
Documento de reserva	Reservation contract
Edificio	Building
En venta	For sale
Escritura de obra nueva y división horizontal	Overall deeds for a new development project
Escritura pública	Public deeds
Estatutos de la comunidad de propietarios	Community bylaws
Expediente de infrición urbanística	Order of urban planning infringement issued by the town hall
Finca	Property
Gastos de comunidad or *cuota de la comunidad de propietarios*	Community of owners' fees
Gestor	A professional who provides administrative services
GIPE (*Asociación Profesional de Gestores Inmobiliarios*)	Professional association of real estate agents
Hacienda	Tax authorities
Hipoteca	Mortgage
IAJD (*Impuesto de Actos Jurídicos Documentados*)	Stamp duty
IBI (*Impuesto sobre Bienes Inmuebles*)	Municipal rates

SPANISH	ENGLISH
IGIC (*Impuesto General Indirecto Canario*)	In the Canaries, a special tax called the General Indirect Tax
IRNR (*Impuesto sobre la renta de no residentes*)	Income tax for non-residents
IRPF (*Impuesto sobre la renta de las personas físicas*)	Income tax
ITP (*Impuesto sobre Transmisiones Patrimoniales*)	Transfer tax
IVA (*Impuesto sobre valor añadido*)	VAT
Ley de costas	Coastal planning law
Ley de ordenación de la edificación	Building regulations law
Ley Reguladora de la Actividad Urbanística (*LRAU*)	'Land grab' law
Libro del edificio	Specifications manual
Licencia de construcción	Planning permission
Licencia de obras or *licencia de reformas*	Building permission
Licencia de primera ocupación	First occupancy licence
Lista de precios	Price list
Estatutos de la comunidad de propietarios	Community of owners' bylaws
Masia	Country property (Catalonia)
Memoria de calidades	Building specifications
Negro	B-money, under-the-table-payments not declared in the deeds
Nota simple informativa	Basic land registry filing
Notario	Public notary
Nueva construcción	New build
Nueva promoción	New development
Número de identidad de extranjero (NIE)	Spanish identity number for foreigners
Patrimonio	Wealth tax
Piso	Flat
Piso y apartamento	Apartment
Plan general	Regional development plan

SPANISH	ENGLISH
Plan parcial	Partial local development plan
Plan urbanístico	Municipal building plan
Planos	Plans
Plusvalía (*Impuesto sobre Incremento del Valor de los Terrenos de Naturaleza Urbana*)	Tax on increases in land values
Poder	Power of attorney
Póliza de seguro	Insurance policy
Projecto	Building project/plans
Promotor	Developer
Proyecto técnico aprobado	Approved technical project
Pueblo	Village
Referencia catastral	Cadastral reference number
Registro de la Propiedad	Land register
Segunda mano	Resale property
Sobre plano	Off-plan
Superficie construida	Built area
Superficie total	Total built area including common areas
Superficie útil	Useable built area
Tasación	Valuation
Tasador	Valuer
Urbana	Residential property
Urbanismo	Town planning department
Urbanización	Residential development
Vendedor	Vendor
Vivienda	Property
Vivienda unifamiliar	Detached property

Need to know more?

General property websites

Association for the Defence of Property Owners
A membership organization that defends the rights of property buyers and owners (only in Spanish).
website: www.adeprovi.com

Country Life Online
Useful information and upmarket properties in Spain.
website: www.countrylife.co.uk

Federation of Overseas Property Developers (FOPDAC)
First Floor
618 Newmarket Road
Cambridge
CB5 8LP
tel: 0870 3501223.
email: enquiries@fopdac.com
website: www.fopdac.com

Foundation Institute of Foreign Property Owners
Organization set up to help buyers and owners.
Apartado 418
03590 Altea
Spain
tel: 00 34 96 584 23 12
fax: 00 34 96 584 15 89
website: www.fipe.org

Practical Spain
Website provides information on relocating permanently to Spain.
website: www.practicalspain.com

Spanish Property Insight
For regional property guides, Spanish property market reports, and everything that you need to help you arrange and manage your property purchase in Spain.
website: www.spanishpropertyinsight.com

Professional organizations

Cadastre online
This useful website enables you to see the basic cadastral details of any property in Spain.
http://ovc.catastro.meh.es

Mortgage Association of Spain
For general information on the mortgage market in Spain.
website: www.ahe.es

Professional Association of Registrars (Land Registry)
Provides useful resources and guides for property buyers in Spain. Expected to be available in English.
website: www.registradores.org

Professional Association of Spanish Lawyers
This website is available only in Spanish. It provides a directory of and links to local legal associations.
website: www.cgae.es

Professional Association of Spanish Notaries
This website includes some guides in English to buying and selling property in Spain, along with other topics of interest.
website: www.notariado.org

Spanish government websites

Directory of Spanish Government Institutions
website: http://www.gksoft.com/govt/en/es.html

Spanish Secretariat of State for Immigration and Emigration
Offers some useful resources for understanding and sorting out the bureaucratic requirements of moving to Spain.
website: http://extranjeros.mtas.es

Spanish Tax Office online (Agencia Tributaria)
The website includes a section in English with guides to the taxes that immigrants and non-residents have to pay when they own property in Spain.
tel: 00 34 91 33 55 33 (Spanish)
website: www.aeat.es

Spanish Tourist Office
PO Box 4009
London W1A 6NB
tel: 020 7486 80 77
email: info.londres@tourspain.es
website: www.tourspain.co.uk

Professional organizations of Spanish estate agents

Agents de la Propiedad Inmobiliaria (API)
Grand Via 66-2
28013 Madrid
Spain
tel: 00 34 91 547 0741
email: cgcoapi@consejocoapis.org
website: www.consejocoapis.org

Associacion Profesional de Gestores Intermediarios en Promociones de Edificaciones (GIPE)
C/Salinas, 6-1°
29015 Malaga
Spain
tel: 00 34 902 11 5295
website: www.gipe.es

Royal Institute of Chartered Surveyors (RICS)
12 Great George Street
Parliament Square
London SW1P 3AD
tel: 020 7222 7000
email: ricsespana@rics.org
website: www.rics.org

Consulates and embassies

British Chamber of Commerce (Spain)
tel: 00 34 93 317 3220
website: www.britishchamberspain.com

British Embassy (Madrid)
Provides some useful guides and contact addresses.
C/ Fernando el Santo 16
28010 Madrid
Spain
tel: 00 34 91 700 8200
website: www.ukinspain.com

Spanish Consulate in London
20 Draycott Place
London SW3 2RZ
tel: 020 7589 8989
website: www.conspalon.org

Airlines

bmi
tel: 0870 607 0555
website: www.bmibaby.com

British Airways
tel: 0870 850 9850
website: www.britishairways.com

easyJet
tel: 0871 750 0100
website: www.easyjet.com

Iberia
tel: 020 8222 8900
website: www.iberia.com

Monarch
tel: 01582 400000
website: www.flymonarch.com

Ryanair
tel: 0871 246 0000
website: www.ryanair.com

Ferries and railways

Brittany Ferries
tel: 08703 665 333
website: www.brittanyferries.co.uk

P & O Ferries
tel: 0870 600 0611
website: www.poferries.com

Red Nacional de Ferrocarriles Españoles (RENFE)
Spanish Railways
website: www.renfe.es

Taking pets abroad

Department for Environment, Food & Rural Affairs
tel: 0870 241 1710
http://www.defra.gov.uk/animalh/quarantine/index.htm

Weather

BBC
www.bbc.co.uk/weather

Other useful websites

Directory Spain
An online directory focused on Spain.
website: www.directoryspain.com

Google Earth
A programme that enables you to see any part of Spain from the air.
website: http://earth.google.com

The International Property Show
International property exhibitions around the UK.
website: www.internationalpropertyshow.com

Magazines and publications

A Place in the Sun's Everything Spain
website: www.everythingspainmag.co.uk

Spanish Homes Magazine
website: www.spanishhomesmagazine.com

Living Spain
website: www.livingspain.co.uk

The Sunday Times Home section
website: www.timesonline.co.uk

Publishers' websites

Blevins Franks
website: www.blevinsfranks.com

HarperCollins Publishers
website: www.collins.co.uk

Survival Books
website: www.survivalbooks.net

Language learning websites

About Spanish
Vocabulary, proverbs, dictionaries, links, etc.
website: http://spanish.about.com

BBC
BBC resources for learning Spanish
website: www.bbc.co.uk/languages/spanish/

Spanish Dictionary
Dictionary of Spanish with audio files.
website: www.spanishdict.com

Spanish lessons
Lessons, vocabulary builder, verb conjugator, exercises, etc.
website: www.donquijote.org/spanishlanguage/

Word Reference
A searchable Spanish dictionary.
website: www.wordreference.com

Further reading

Books

The Blevins Franks Guide to Living in Spain
(Blevins Franks)
Buying a Home in Spain, David Hampshire
(Survival Books)
Buying Property Abroad, Jeremy Davies
(Which? Books)
Collins Desktop Spanish Dictionary
(HarperCollins Publishers)
Collins Easy Learning Spanish Grammar
(HarperCollins Publishers)
Collins Need to Know? Speak Spanish
(HarperCollins Publishers)
Collins Spanish Phrase Book & Dictionary
(HarperCollins Publishers)

Living and Working in Spain, David Hampshire
(Survival Books)
Making a Living in Spain, Anne Hall
(Survival Books)
The Best Places to Buy a Home in Spain,
Joanna Styles (Survival Books)

Maps

2006 Map of Spain & Portugal 0 00 720565 1
(HarperCollins Publishers)
Collins Road Atlas Spain & Portugal 0 00 720562 7
(HarperCollins Publishers)
Collins Road Map Spain & Portugal 0 00 719706 3
(HarperCollins Publishers)

Index

◌ **Collins** need to know?

Look out for these recent titles in Collins' practical and accessible need to know? series.

To order any of these titles, please telephone 0870 787 1732. For further information about all Collins books, visit our website: www.collins.co.uk